'I have to tell you now that no such undertaking has been received, and that consequently this country is at war with Germany.'

Neville Chamberlain
Prime Minister
3 September, 1939

i

An early picture of Hedon School showing the Bull Ring. Girls used to do 'tipple-overs' on the iron railings which were removed during the war for scrap.

TEN O'CLOCK SCHOLARS

Wartime Reminiscences and Records of Pupils and Staff of HEDON SCHOOL

Collected, Compiled and Edited

by

Margaret and Bob Cochrane

[Log Book: 'July 5, 1940. The L.E.A.'s rule of opening school at 10 a.m., if the All Clear siren goes after midnight, received today']

Highgate of Beverley

Highgate Press (Markham) Limited 1995

By the same authors
Death Comes to Hedon (The cholera epidemic of 1849)

British Library Cataloguing in Publication Data.
A catalogue record for this book is available from the British Library.

ISBN   1   899498   02   8

Published by

Highgate of Beverley
Highgate Press (Markham) Limited
24 Wylies Road, Beverley, HU17 7AP
Telephone (01482) 866826

Printed by

ba/print

4 Newbegin, Lairgate, Beverley, HU17 8EG
Telephone (01482) 886017

Cover Picture: the 'Red Cross Pig': see page 62.

Contents

Preface

When Margaret and Bob Cochrane approached me about the idea of producing a book about the lives of children at Hedon School during wartime, I thought that it would certainly be a worthwhile project which would be of great interest to pupils past, present and indeed the future

The anecdotes contained within the following pages, some serious, some humorous, give a real insight into the lives and feelings of the children at that time.

I was interested to read, on a professional level, how an organisation, such as a school, continued to operate in spite of the stresses and hardships that occurred in these difficult years.

Many reminiscences will be shared and many words will no doubt be written to commemorate the 50th anniversary of the end of the war and now, with this book, there is an interesting and permanent record of a significant period in the history of Hedon.

My thanks and congratulations go to Margaret and Bob for the time and commitment they have given in compiling this splendid account.

Paul Rimmer
Headteacher, Hedon County Primary School

The Book

This book has been compiled from two sources: firstly, the reminiscences of former pupils and staff and, secondly, the School logbooks. We have arranged and edited these sources and it is our intention, as far as possible, to let them speak for themselves.

The School

Hedon School was an all-age school catering for children from four-to five-years old until their 14th birthday. School numbers varied, but were about 280, including infants, who were taught in a separate building of corrugated iron construction, known locally as the Tin Tabernacle.

Although nominally part of the school, the Infants Department was treated as a separate entity with one of the three teachers as Headmistress. They kept a separate log book. The building was situated off Stockwell Lane, where the present Hedon County Primary School now stands, and consisted of two classrooms, one each side of an entrance foyer and cloakroom. The larger classroom held two classes. The school was heated by two stoves, later three. There was no artificial lighting until after the war; the caretaker was given a bicycle lamp to help on winter mornings. There were outside earth toilets across a rough gravel playground and scrubbed knees were common. The number of infants was around 70 – 80.

The main school was in the old Board School which housed juniors and seniors. Standards I -IV (juniors) had separate classes. The seniors were taught in two classes, Standards V & VIb in one, and Standards VIa, VII and ExVII in another. The pressure was relieved by some of the seniors transferring to Withernsea. Classes were over 30. In 1939 numbers were 223, ten fewer than the maximum that could be accommodated, in what were very cramped premises. The boys and girls had separate playgrounds, and P.T., Maypole Dancing and other outside activities were performed there or on Market Hill. There were outside toilets. Electricity had only been installed in 1939.

The Town

Hedon in wartime was like an armed camp. There were road blocks on the roads in and out of Hedon where the road was narrowed to the width of one vehicle. The town was surrounded by the defences of the Humber and Hull: searchlights, barrage balloons, anti-aircraft and rocket batteries. Troops were stationed in the district, at first, to prevent a possible invasion, later preparing and practising for their own invasion of Europe. Houses were used as billets and camps of Nissen huts were built in the area, the one down Ivy Lane within a stone's throw of the Infants School.

In spite of all this activity, school life went on with surprisingly little disruption. Staff and pupils alike took upheaval in their stride and got on with their job.

1939 Members of Staff

Infant School: Mrs E. Smith to October 31, 1939
Mrs E.O.Grainger (Temporary Head)
Miss N.M.Elletson
Miss L.Stephenson
On January 1, 1940 Miss F. Rawle became Headmistress.

Junior and Senior School

August 21st Re-opened School at 9 a.m.

Miss J. Anderson has obtained a post at the new Hessle Junior School, and her services at this school terminate. Miss F. J. Cass, College Trained Certificated Teacher, leaving College July 1939, is appointed Assistant Mistress at this School, commencing today.

The present staff is as follows.

Junior I. Miss F. J. Cass. Cert. Room 2.
Junior II Miss F. Farnaby. Cert. Room 4
Junior III Mr H. Cox Cert. Room 5
Junior IV. Miss M. Beedham Cert. Room 1.
Senior I. VIb. Mr V. G. Skelton Cert. Room 3
Senior II. VIIa Ex.VII. Mr F.D. Lacey. Cert. Room 6
Head Teacher. Cert. S.T.Johnson.
Accommodation 235. On roll 223.
Present this morning 208.
Scholars left of age. 11. Scholarship 1.
Left to other schools. 4.

Mr. and Mrs. S. T. Johnson

Mr. Sidney Johnson (known to the boys as 'Gaffer' Johnson) was the Headmaster of Hedon School throughout the war years. He had served in the First World War and, prior to the Second, had been on a course on gas and air raid precautions. Shortly after the War broke out he was appointed Sub-Controller in the A.R.P. with responsibility for co-ordinating precautions and rescue services over a wide area of Holderness around Hedon. He received the M.B.E. for his wartime services.

In 1941 he became Mayor of Hedon, a position which he held for six years. He was also a J.P., a Haven Commissioner, and, in later years, an Honorary Freeman of Hedon.

3

Evacuation Plans.

June 19" Received from the L.E.A. particulars of children evacuation scheme for Hedon, as a plan in preparation, asking for suggestions for accommodation for 180 scholars.

July 3rd Mr. Moffatt, County Council Inspector, called at 10.0 a.m. With the Head Teacher, he visited and inspected premises suggested for the accommodation of 180 evacuated children in the proposed plan for Hedon. Returning at 11.20, he visited Junior Form I and the class teacher, Miss Anderson. Afterwards he visited other classes.

Aug. 21st The proposal for bringing 180 child evacuees to Hedon, in the event of war, is not to be proceeded with, and no further arrangements are to be made. (Authority of L.E.A. by letter).

How I heard about the war

We knew there was going to be a war. There'd been scares about it before but this time it looked serious. We listened to the broadcast on Sunday morning and heard Chamberlain make the announcement.

My brother was in the Territorials and I knew, from talking in the family and from when he was called up, that there was likely to be a war.

My brother was called up a few days before war broke out so I knew that something was going to happen.

When they put the siren up at the Town Hall, I thought something was happening. My dad was in the ambulance service and he knew war was coming.

I remember my Mum being overjoyed when Chamberlain came back with his little piece of paper. When the war happened I heard about it on the wireless and in the papers as well.

My aunts used to talk about a war. Then one day at school I remember the Headmaster coming into the classroom and whispering something to Miss Cass. They both looked very strange. Then we were all sent home. I think the date was Friday 1 September, 1939. War was declared on Sunday.

I was never aware there was going to be a war. I think I was too young. The first thing I knew was when somebody said we were having one.

I heard about the war on the wireless and my family talked about it. My eldest brother had maps and everything.

The Church bells were supposed to ring at 11 a.m. if war was declared. We were all at Sunday School listening for them but the bells never went. We came out at 11.15 and, as we were coming home, a man told us war had been declared.

I remember the day most vividly. My father coming in on the Sunday morning and saying we all had to be quiet. I was one of a big family and my sister, she was just a baby, and I was holding her. I can remember the wireless being switched on and the announcement made by Mr. Chamberlain. It was so serious and for the first time in my life I remember that we had complete silence. It was a very solemn moment.

My sister was in the choir at Hedon Church and came home and told us. It had been given out in the Church. It didn't mean a lot to me then, I was only eight.

I think we just took it for granted that a war was coming and then it arrived. I think the atmosphere was that a war was coming.

As we came out of Sunday School, somebody told us that the war had started. We thought it was exciting, and we were cheering and laughing shouting, 'We're going to have a go at the Jerries. We'll show 'em.'

We were all expecting a war. I used to see the barrage balloons and when they first came I knew something was going to happen. Then we heard about it on the radio.

They put sandbags up before the war started and some of the men had to go away to the army or navy so we guessed something was up.

I was walking home from Church and a man told me war had been declared. I ran all the way then.

1938

Sept. 30. | Air Raid Precautions circular received from E.R.E.A.

Sept. 27. | J. V. G. Skelton, B.Sc. took charge of this school today. The head master Mr S. Johnson will be absent for some days.

Oct. 6th | Head Teacher resumed duty after attending a special course in A.R.P. duties.

1939

Sept. 1st Closed at noon today

Sept 4th | Government closure of one week on the outbreak of war between Great Britain and Germany.

Sept. 6th | Cancellation of medical inspection.

Sept 7th | Cancellation of proposed Physical Training Course for staff at Willerby.

Sept. 9th | Outdoor painting of the school premises has been continued this week by Messrs. Moody, of Hedon.

Sept. 11th | Re-opened school this morning at 9 A.M. As a school in a neutral area, no evacuees are being received now.

Sept. 11th | Ordinary time table suspended today, to allow of detailed organisation of school air raid precautions, and practice in same.

We were in Sunday School, at the Chapel in George Street, and, halfway through, somebody came in and said something to Mr. Mitchell and he went out. When we went home he was building a wall outside the police station, which was where the library is now. They built it right up over the windows.

That Sunday I was brambling with my sister on the way to Paull when we saw the balloons go up and the siren went. That was on 3rd September. My father always said there was going to be a war.

I'd been to Sunday School and the siren went that morning and of course I was trying to be brave – it was a most awful sound. Shortly afterwards the all-clear went and somebody told me it was just a test.

I had only started teaching at the school a few days when the war started. The school closed for a week after the declaration. I went across to what was Brooksbank's garage to fill sandbags. That was my introduction to war – navvying! It was something positive to do. Then nothing much happened for some time – almost an anticlimax.

I remember it clearly. It was Sunday lunch time and by the afternoon all our family had gone off to stay with relatives at Beeford. I think they thought the bombs were going to drop straight away. We stayed six weeks.

We moved from Paull to Hedon at the start of the war as my Dad was going into the Army. He thought it would be safer for us and better to be near his family who lived in Hedon.

My family were expecting the war and so we listened and heard the announcement on the radio. I was listening to it with my Mum and thought, 'What happens now?' Mother listened to it all and after it was over sent me to my Grandmother's with something. I didn't want to go – we'd just declared war – so I said, 'What if the bombers come while I'm going?'. She said, ' Oh they won't. You'll be alright. You've got your identity bracelet on.' I went, but I was really scared.

The first night of the war the sirens went. My dad was in the A.F.S. and was out at the time and he rattled on the back door. We lived in George Street at the time – the air raid siren was going nearly mad in the back garden – and there was Len Sharpe hammering like hell on the front door (he was calling my dad out). We were frightened to death.

The first time I realised there was a war on and what it meant was when the sirens went while we were in school and a mother rushed in, in a panic, to take her child home.

1939
Aug 21st

a plan for air raid action for this school has been drawn up. At present there are no refuges, no shelters, and no sandbag protection. All children have been warned to obtain gas masks and to take proper care of them.

Sept 12

Yesterday and today the Head Teacher, holding L.A.G.C, instructed all the scholars present at school, in groups of ten at a time, in the use and care of a gas respirator.

Sept. 13

Councillor A. Moody, local A.R.P. Officer, called with regard to A.R.P. and air raid warning, and also deficiencies in childrens respirators, which had been reported to him.

Sept. 14th

This afternoon, from 1.45 to 4.0, the respirator of every child in the school was tested for fitting and breathing, by the Head Teacher and Mr. H.H. Lambert, L.A.G.C. Instructor, of Hedon. About 16 out of 170 were found to be in need of attention at the depôt.

Gas Masks

Ocky Rawson was the Town Crier. He used to come round with a bell shouting about jumble sales and things. I remember him shouting that we had to go to the Town Hall to get our gas masks.

We had to go to the Town Hall for our gas masks. I went with my little brother. That Council Chamber in the Town Hall was painted a horrible colour – it was green or brown and cream.

I was only little and I had a Mickey Mouse gas mask with a floppy nose. Later it was changed for a bigger one.

We got our gas masks at the Town Hall. I don't remember where we got our identity cards but I can still remember the number – JCHA 1654.

We went, family by family, to the Town Hall to be fitted out. Mine wouldn't fit me and I had to have the next size. I hated it, having something over my face like that.

We did have gas mask practice at school to show the infants how to put them on. Most children could manage but some of them needed a little help. They always had to bring them to school. It's surprising how soon they became used to them.

We used to try them on at school, at first for a short time but, gradually, for longer and longer so we got used to them.

We had to put on our gas masks in school to see how quickly we could do it. Once we had to sit and wear them for so long – it was horrible – some children almost panicked.

We practised in school. We thought it was rather amusing really.

They tested them at school with a piece of cardboard. You put it underneath and you had to breathe in and hold it there by suction to show that the air was coming through the filter and not round the sides.

Mr Johnson did the gas masks. We kept our identity cards in our gas mask boxes. When we put them on we must have looked hideous or very comical but nobody laughed. When the teacher looked at us I wonder how she kept her face straight.

The smell when you put it on – I remember saying, 'I can't wear this, I can't wear this.'

I didn't like my gas mask at all – having something over my face and breathing in it – rubbery like – ugh!

A bit of a lark really – it beat lessons.

It was a horrible feeling putting it on I thought – I thought I was going to smother.

It was the smell I hated.

I didn't really worry about wearing my gas mask.

I'd never seen anything like them in my life. You just had to get used to them. They used to sweat up inside. You could make rude noises if you blew down them.

The first time I heard the siren when I was in school, I went to put on my gas mask. I thought you had to put it on as soon as you heard the siren. As a child you'd been given it and told about it so that's what you did. I was surprised to find you didn't.

1940

April 16th Alderman Moody, Chief of Hedon A.R.P. Services, the Head Teacher and Mr. V. G. Skelton inspected the gas respirator of every child present in school today and tested the fitting. Eighteen cases were notified for attention at 6 P.M. at the depot.

Oct. 20th Gas mask inspection, overhauling and practice.

1942

April 2o Examination of all respirators and air raid warning practices during this week.

May 18th The A.R.P warden visited during afternoon to examine the childrens gas masks. 4 were found to be defective.

* I DENOTES INFANT LOG BOOK

1943

Nov. 4 The number of air raid alerts at night has very considerably diminished during the past few months, and respirators are no longer carried about or brought to school.

10

What I couldn't understand was that if they dropped gas, it was too ruddy late to put your gas mask on.

If you came to school without it, you had to go home for your gas mask and you got into trouble.

We carried them in cardboard boxes with a string to start with, then some people started having fancy cases made out of leatherette. We took them everywhere to start with , but, later on, near the end of the war, we didn't bother.

Some people made covers for their boxes out of sort of brown material so they would keep dry in the rain.

I had a really glamorous cover on my gas mask case.

At first my gas mask was in a cardboard box, but later I had a sort of triangular shaped, sort of imitation leather one.

The kids used to get your gas mask and chase about with it and wave it about.

I didn't like it , but we never had to use them properly, thank God.

Anti-gas training certificate. Mr. Johnson, the Head, had atttended a similar course in 1938.

1939

July 7 Mr. B. Stamford, County Architect, called at 3.50 with regard to School Air raid precaution and action. His suggestions were carefully noted.

Aug. 28 Interviews with local A.R.P. officials with regard to arrangements, if any, for protection of school children at Hedon in case of air raids.

Aug. 22nd A staff meeting was held, as arranged, this evening, all members being present. Among the subjects discussed were :- Arithmetic Written Work, System of Marking, Team System, Prefects and Leaders, Time Table, Points of Discipline, Group Work and Specialisation, Organised Games, And Air Raid Precautions in School. A meeting of the Parents' Committee was arranged for next week.

Sept 11" In air raid precautions for school, those who can reach home in 7 minutes are being sent home and the others are escorted into the fields in Ivy Lane, and placed in groups under the hedges.

Shelter

The East Riding County Council area was, in contrast to Hull, considered a low risk area and funds for spending on protective measures for schools were limited. The Education Committee, therefore, decided that provision of air raid shelters all-round was impracticable. They voted to spend £1,482 on other measures to protect from blast and splinters, with a further £1000 for contingencies (A.R.P. sub-committee Minute September 14, 1939). This was for all schools in their control. Hedon's share at the Mixed School was a blast wall and tape for the windows and also tape for the windows at the Infants School. This was in spite of the fact that a previous meeting of the Education Committee in July had considered schools in Hedon and Haltemprice to be particularly vulnerable.

For a meeting of the full County Council to be held on February 2, 1940, Councillor Drewery had tabled the motion: 'That in the opinion of this Council, the air raid shelter accommodation agreed and provided for school children in Hedon is inadequate and the sub-committee which deals with this question be instructed to take immediate steps to provide improved accommodation against air raid risks at these schools.'

The motion was withdrawn because action to improve the situation was being taken before the meeting came round. Air raid shelters were to be built at the two schools at a cost of £348. 18s for Hedon Mixed School and £290.3.2d for the Infants, due to be completed by April. Whether the very fact of the tabling of the motion had anything to do with the decision or whether it is just a coincidence is a matter of conjecture.

The only photograph we have been able to trace of the Infants School, known locally as the 'Tin Tabernacle'.

Sept. 12th
1939

Consent of parents is obtained in every case of a child being sent home under air raid precaution.

Sept. 12

Interviews with a large number of parents, yesterday and today, on the question of protection for the children in A.R.P. at school.

In 24 cases of absence, parents decline to send children until adequate protection in A.R.P. is provided.

This is being reported to the L.E.A.

Sept 12

Wrote to the L.E.A. on A.R.P. protection for children at school.

Oct. 2nd

The County Architect, (Mr. B. Stamford) and the Clerk of works (Mr C.W. Stephenson) visited this afternoon to arrange for immediate Air Raid Protection schemes for the schools. It was decided to arrange for work to be done at the school so that children would not have to be taken into the fields during an air raid. The question of numbers was considered, as also were questions of suitable rooms and the number of Infants who would come to this school for protection.

After the war started they gave us a 'pep talk' at school. We had to see how long it took us to run home and, if it took us longer than a certain time, we had to stay at school during a warning. We all said it took us only a few minutes because we wanted to be at home if there was anything doing.

At first a lot of wooden beams were put up in the boys' cloakroom. I suppose it was kind of a blast wall really.

All the windows had to have tape put on them in a criss-cross pattern. Some had a kind of rubber glue and net stuck on. Some of the older boys and teachers did it. Clive Hunter who used to be on Radio Humberside went to Hedon school. He played the accordion. He was helping to put protection on the tall windows and the ladder slipped when he was at the top. He fell off and landed with a thump. It was a great laugh. I don't think he hurt himself, nobody seemed bothered much.

When the siren went, if we could get home in so long, we could go home. We had to practise that a time or two, to prove we could do it. We ran very fast because we were sort of borderline, but we could do it. It took a lot longer to get back!

I didn't go in the shelter, I used to run home. If you lived at school near the beginning they used to let you, but later on the parents said it was dangerous and everybody had to stay at school.

I was one of those who ran home when the siren went. I was always very frightened. I never ran back so fast.

The School Air Raid Shelter is still there, although bricked up. View from Souttergate, the roof of the school can be seen in the background.

1939

Oct. 20[13th] During this week's holiday closure, air raid protection work is being carried out by joiners and builders.

1940

Jan. 25 Mr. B. Stanford, County Architect and Mr. W.H. Stephenson, Clerk of Works. No 2 Area visited from noon to 12.45 at the school on A.R.P. and proposed air raid shelters outside.

Feb. 9 Visits paid this week by the County Architect and Clerk of Works with regard to the provision of outdoor air raid shelters at both schools at Hedon.

Mar. 1 Workmen commence operations on the outside school air raid shelter site.

April 20 Work is proceeding rapidly on the construction of the school air raid shelter. Frequent visits are made to the school by the Clerk of Works, the County Architect and officials. The boys' playground is being used by the workmen for store and workshop and we are making the best of the circumstances for physical training and recreation.

When the siren went, my two sisters came over from the other school and ran me home because the shelter at the tin school hadn't been built just then.

It put the fear of God into you when the siren went. It frightened you more than anything, that wailing sound. You didn't know what to expect – if the Germans were coming or what.

We were just round the corner from the school so we could go home if a warning went. Me and my pals didn't go home – we went into my granny's yard and had a smoke and a bit of a lark. Sometimes we only had one cigarette and passed it round. We used to get them from a machine at the post office – it was twopence for two cigarettes and three matches – that's old pennies – less than a penny in new money. We would watch the planes out of the cowshed. We reckoned we could tell which was which.

I remember running home when the siren went. One day I set off and, when I was halfway across Market Hill, there was a girl behind me, standing there and crying her eyes out. I shouted, 'Come on! RUN!', but she wouldn't, so I went back and grabbed her hand and dragged her. She came in the end but it made me late and my mother had been worried and set off to meet me. That particular time an aircraft did come over. I was looking at everybody's gardens as we ran past to see if we were big enough to jump over the wall if it came back.

At first, if the siren went, we all marched to Styche's field and Ivy Lane and sat under the trees. The teachers were very strict and made each class keep together and keep quiet.

At the beginning of the war we all went and sat under the trees down Ivy Lane. When I asked the teacher why, she said we would be safe there because the trees would keep the bombs off us. I couldn't see how a few leaves and twigs were going to do much good.

Before the air raid shelter was constructed, we used to take the children out under the trees, down Ivy Lane, just past the Vicarage. The Nissen huts had not yet been built. Each class had its own designated area. I used to call it, 'Hedging and ditching'. I thought it was, and probably it sounded, mad, but we were all expecting bombs and it was probably the best thing that could be done. If we were all congregated in one area and something dropped on or near the school, it could have been carnage. This way, if anything happened, the children were all spread out and could not all be hit at the same time. It was a temporary arrangement, and, as such, did seem hilarious, but, on sitting back and thinking about it, what is the alternative?. What really worried me was, 'Suppose it rained and the ditches were full.'

When the air raid warning went, we picked up our goods and chattels and took the children up to the Mixed School, down the street with all these little tots. Eventually they built an air raid shelter at the back of the tin school – a brick air raid shelter with two chemical toilets in it. It was the best building we had. The only toilets we'd had before were earth closets across the yard for the children. We used to go in the shelter and sing and suchlike. Later on they made an extra door in the back of the largest classroom. We used to open that door and flock through there.

It was dark, musty and gloomy in the shelter. It was built in the garden of Painter's Cottages and half under the playground. They put a bike shed on top. Sometimes girls took their knitting . We all sang and knitted until the all clear. I remember going in the shelter but not for an air raid. Every week we went in.

The new air raid shelter was in bays and each class was allocated a particular area. It was

1940

April 30" Acceptance for care of material for the school air raid shelter consisting of 3 chemical lavatories, one porcelain wash basin, three electric lamps and cable with three keys

May 10" Frequent air raid drill taken during School hours this week using the school air raid shelter.

May 15" Chairman of managers called to inspect air raid shelter. Vicar also called for this purpose. Expressed their dissatisfaction are with emergency lighting.

I

May 17" County Architect called with extra electric lamps for air raid shelter. We have now 5 large lamps and 3 cycle lamps.

I

Nov. 5 Children taken to shelter for 50 minutes during afternoon air-raid warning. The shelter - roof is extremely wet, and drips constantly on the clothes are of the children as they sit round the walls

I

certainly better than 'hedging and ditching'. We often had singing in there . It was too dark to read. I can remember one time they sang so loudly, and so merrily, that I didn't hear the all clear go. The next time they sang loudly on purpose and someone said, 'Keep it going, lads.'

The shelter had a concrete top. We went down to it. It was like a bunker really. We were glad to get out.

The shelter was divided into bays with wooden slatted forms round. Each class always sat in the same place. There were four or five bays with no doors in between. When it was an air raid or a practice, teacher blew a whistle and we all marched in.

It was dark and dismal. There were only little lights, maybe battery lights. Sometimes they told us stories and we used to sing.

I had to stay at school if there was a warning because I couldn't get home in time. When the shelter was built we went in there . It was a lark. It was very dark in there. We had some fun with the girls.

It was dark. We took our gas-masks. We were always told you collected that and left everything else behind. I didn't like it in there – there were so many in there. It was very crowded and claustrophobic.

I didn't think the school shelter was as bad as those Anderson things – not so claustrophobic.

Horrible – damp, miserable and cold.

The air raid shelter had a funny smell. Everybody said it was horrible.

I was in the Infants. I can't remember the shelter but I can remember going out of a special little door to get to it. I don't think it was as high as an ordinary door, more like a hatch.

We all followed teacher out of the classroom, down into the shelter. It was dark and full – a bit of laugh really – you know what it's like when there's a crowd of you!

At first I went home – I lived in George Street but I still had to practise going in the shelter. I hated it – it was horrible. It was low and damp with bare brick walls. There was a funny feeling about it.

People told frightening stories, especially the boys. I was scared going in there, it really was spooky.

I don't remember a toilet in the shelter – I suppose if you needed to go you'd have to run to the ones in the yard and never mind the bombs.

At night time my Dad was in charge of the school air raid shelter and when the bombing got bad a lot of people used to go in there. We went with him sometimes.

I didn't like getting up if there was an air raid. I stopped in bed if I could. Dad used to shout at me, 'Get up or I'll slap your arse', but I usually stayed.

1940

March 20th | Planning of work at the school garden. The Infant's school air raid shelter will take up one plot previously used for vegetable growing

July 30 | Staff have been asked by Architects' department to tape all windows with paper tape.

Sept 9th 1940 | During the holiday all the windows and screen glass have been painted with a preparation furnished by the L.E.A Architects' Dept. and have had strips of thick paper pasted over them. This work has been done voluntarily by the men teachers and senior boys.

Sept 9' | The School air raid shelter is now ready for use and exercises are commenced in air raid precautions with the Scholars.

Sept. 30 | The school air raid shelter is open to the public after school hours and during the night. Shelter wardens have been appointed.

October 1941 – Class SV in front of bike shed/air raid shelter: Miss M. Beedham (Shortly before she left)

Boys – Back Row: Charlie Higginson, David Panton, Jimmy Hurd, Eric Kelsey, Geoff Barrow, Cec Hunter, Eric Lee, Stuart Beadle.
Front Row: Bill Tong, Gordon Cripps, Michael Wickner, Keith Craven, Colin Parker, Arthur Brooks, Bobby Wray, Walter Johnson.

Girls – Standing: Eva Tong, Ethel Thompson.

Back Row: Sheila Saunders (now Dickinson), Brenda Greenwood, Beryl Rennardson (now French), Megan Ketley (now Glenn), Margaret Taylor (now Margaret Parker), Betty Morrell, Lilian Fewlass (now Swainger).
Front Row: Gwen Betts, Pam Brockman, Shirley Atkinson (now Coleman), Elsie Mannering (now Richardson), Mary Blenkinsop, Audrey Britton.

21

1939

Aug. 25 Classes for 20 Senior girls for domestic science and 20 Senior Boys for woodwork at Bilton are being formed. Conveyance is by private car from Johnson's Garage.

Aug. 28 Notice received that the woodwork class will not be held at present as the Master, Mr Kirk, is serving with the Territorials.

Sept. 1st This afternoon Mr H. Cox and Mr F.D. Lacey volunteered for war service at Hull R.A.F. depôt.

Sept. 14th Notice received from L.E.A. that all Cookery and Woodwork classes are suspended. This will necessitate a revision of the school time-table.

Sept. 19th The Head Teacher spoke to the Senior boys and girls this morning on Calmness and carrying on one's duties in war time.

Disruptions and Shortages

Before the war, we used to go to Withernsea, the girls, for cookery lessons, but after that, of course, they wouldn't let us go. We used to go on the ordinary service buses.

Some of us older boys used to go to Bilton for woodwork classes. We went in cars from Johnson's Garage. When the war started they stopped that because Mr. Kirk, the teacher, was called up with the territorials.

They used to let us out of school to watch the Holderness Hunt meet, but the war put a stop to that.

I used to run in the relay team. We used to have sports days where we went round the schools, but it ended when the war came and we were not allowed to travel.

I had three school journeys, three good ones, Wales, London and the Lake District, but these stopped with the war. My younger sister didn't get any.

I was in the last football team championship. The final was played at Leven where we beat a team from Brandesburton and Tickton combined and won the Holderness Schools Shield for the second year running and the fourth time in seven years. After that they stopped having them. I don't remember playing at all during the war. I suppose we kept the shield for the duration.

I remember going to London before the war but it was the only school trip we got because then they stopped them.

My sister who's older than me went on school outings but I never got any because of the war. I couldn't go to Withernsea for cookery either.

Just after the war started Mr. Lacey who took the top class got called up and Mr. Cox took the top class so I got Mr. Cox twice.

At the start of the war teacher asked if anyone wanted to be evacuated to Canada. I put my hand up. My sister ran home and shouted, 'Mam, Mam, he's going to Canada, he's going to Canada.' The next day she was round at school and that was the end of that. Later I heard that the boat I would have gone on , if I'd been given a place, had been sunk.

Paper was in very short supply. We were told to write across the margins in our exercise books. Once we tried writing on the normal lines and then turned the books round and started writing across the other way but they stopped that – you could hardly read it.

With our exercise books we weren't allowed to waste any paper whatsoever. We had to write on the inside cover, in the margins and on the inside and the outside of the back cover.

It was difficult getting stock. The stock room was the Holy of Holies. You put in a little requisition – Can I have three crayons – No! Stock was short. The stock room was the Headmaster's sanctum. You went up a little folding ladder to get into it. We had to be very careful. We used the same text books all the time; we had to make them last. We used to put backs on the books. We used old boxes for cardboard in craft, scrounged from various sources. We were poverty-stricken by today's standards. When I look at what is happening nowadays I feel there is tremendous waste.

You just hadn't to waste anything – and paper – we were given books and every line had to be used – even if you started your day's work on the bottom line. It had to be used. Since

1939

Sept. 19ᵗ Mr H.H. Lambert of The Hall, Hedon, called today with regard to the Senior girls joining classes for national service in sewing, knitting, making bandages, pads, and swabs. She spoke to the assembled girls for about fifteen minutes.

Oct. 23ʳᵈ Mr F.D. Lacey joined H.M. Army today. Head Teacher took the Senior Class today. VI.A, VII, and Ex.VII. Education Authority notified by telephone.

Oct. 25ᵗ The change in staff will necessitate a change in specialisation and a revision of the time-table. Details now being worked out.

Nov. 21ˢᵗ Afternoon session changed from today from 1.15 to 3.45 to 1.0 to 3.15. (black-out 4.25) to allow for cleaning. This to continue until after the Christmas closure.

Nov. 24 The senior tops have listened to two wireless talks by Professor Ogilvie on World Affairs, each on Thursday

Hedon School had a good reputation for football, winning the Holderness Shield many times. This is a photograph of their winning team at the end of the 1938-9 season. Due to travel restrictions matches could not be played during the war so presumably they remained champions for five years!

At the back: S. T. Johnson and Harold Cox.

Back Row: Jim Laidlaw, Dick Mannering, Bill Panton, Bill Tullock, Phil Hales, Ted Burnham, Ken Slaughter.

Front Row: Ernie Wilkinson, Harold Lilley, Eric Smith, Phil Everingham, Roy Rooney.

1940

Jan 9" The Seniors listened from 3.45 today to the Prime Minister's speech by wireless.

1941

July 4: During recent months the school has been freely used as a Rest Centre at night for the public and for people from Hull. Food and blankets are stored and a staff take over duty at night, providing tea and comforts. Times are usually 7.30pm to 7.0 a.m. The record number was 238.

1943

Sept. 24: The school is used two evenings a week for Army Cadet Corps Training, one evening for Church Choir Practice, one evening for Church Tennis Club Winter Session, and on Sunday afternoon for Church Sunday School. It is not now used for Home Guard Training, A.T.C training and lectures, or as the headquarters of the Special Constables, or for Civil Defence. It is earmarked as a Rest Centre and there are stores of blankets, emergency articles and food here then I've always been careful, saving bits of string and wrapping paper where these can be used again.

In art classes, we couldn't get materials, so the art class was repairing text books because they couldn't get new ones. We had to take wallpaper or brown paper to school to cover the books and we had to stick the spines back.

We couldn't get proper material for needlework and I had to make a pillow case out of some very hard stuff. You couldn't get the needle through. I always ended up with blood on my fingers by the end of the lesson. I was always in trouble because the stitches weren't right.

I never went to gardening because I had special duties. I had to look after the stores – books, pencils and things. All these were in very short supply. I must have been honoured because Mr. Johnson trusted me. He wouldn't let anyone else have the key.

The old school stoves were a bit of a pest. When we ran out of coke we had lessons in our overcoats. Those high ceilings in the classrooms took out all the heat. The coldest place was in the cloakroom. No hot water to wash your hands or wash out the pots after a painting lesson.

One winter when it was very cold and the heating wasn't working, Mr. Skelton asked every child to bring one piece of coal from home so we could have a fire in the classroom. He even used the bits of paper we brought it in, so at least we kept warm for one day.

We had fires in school. My dad caught me collecting firewood. He went in and played hell because we had not done any lessons for about a week. We had been sent out to collect what we could because there was no fuel for the fires in the classrooms.

Three of us were detailed off as errand boys when the men got called up. We didn't have to be at school till 9.30 and then we could leave early to go and work at the shops. We didn't volunteer, we were detailed off by Mr. Johnson but we didn't mind as it got us out of school and we got paid, but not much

When there'd been a long raid at night we were allowed to go in late. Sometimes all of the children didn't turn up – you could understand that when they'd been up half the night. We had some quite small classes sometimes but it was amazing how little they seemed to be affected.

At one stage in about 1941 the siren used to go every night. The next morning we were allowed to go in later.

In 1941 a large number of people came out of Hull to escape the severe bombing which continued for some months. Some people came permanently and put up shacks on Bond's Estate or stayed with relatives. Others came each night, sleeping in the school, chapel, with relatives or friends and even in the fields. This exodus from Hull seems to have made a great impression on many of the children of the time.

I can see them now, each night hordes of people came streaming out of Hull, some walking, some cycling, some on horses and carts or lorries, all with little bundles, anything to escape the bombing.

My father was in charge of all the evacuees who came out of Hull to this area, and they used to come out every night. A lot of them walked or cycled and some slept in the school. We couldn't go in until blankets and everything had been cleared up and it was cleaned. If you were early you had to shake blankets. I can remember them all walking and cycling out.

1941

To Infants School   JULY 15/41
         HEDON   33

I
         100 Blankets
         1 Sachet
       x 2 Water Bottles   1 Shovel
         1 Field Boiler 1 Ladle
         1 Kettle 36 Cups
         12 T Spoons   2 Knives
         2 Tea Pots   2 Buckets
       o 1 Wash Bowl 1 Tin Opener
       o 3 Tea Cloths 3 Dish Cloths
         3 Face Cloths 12 Towels
         12 Sanitary Towels 12 Napkins
         3 Feeding Bottles 1 Medical Box
         1 Bar Soap Toilet Soap 6x½
         1 Disenfectant 4 Toilet Rolls
         12 P.C. 1 Notice 1 Chamber (unexamined)

                 J Rawll
         REC'D July 15 1941
               DATE

Emergency supplies deliverd to the Infants School.

October 1941. Mr. Cox taught Standards VIa, VII and Ex VII altogether as form SII. Illustration above shows the whole form. Illustration below and on page 33 show the separate groups.

Class Ex VII. Back Row: Clive Hunter, Bill Panton. Front Row: Norma ----?, Mary Wilkinson, Hilda Mablethorpe, June Hornsey, ----?

1940

Jan. 10" Requisitions for stationery and needlework supplies, in which we are at present short, sent to L. E. A.

Feb. 12th School supply of coke exhausted before arrival of next order. After telephone conversation with County Hall, efforts made to obtain supply locally. Regular order is behind schedule delivery. 5. 0. p. m Two tons of coke obtained from Finney's of Hull.

Jan 18"
I Have sent a message to plumber re water pipes which have flooded the cloakroom. Plumber removed pipes.

Feb 14"
I No water pipes yet. Lack of water is causing serious inconvenience both to staff and visiting officers (dental and medical)

1941

Oct 3
1941
I The heating stove has not yet been put together. It was taken to pieces in the holidays.

couldn't go in until blankets and everything had been cleared up and it was cleaned. If you were early you had to shake blankets. I can remember them all walking and cycling out. Then at five o'clock in the morning they all started getting up to go back to Hull.

People were sleeping in the school. They brought their family along; they brought their food; they brought their pets. Next morning we had to wait until it was cleaned out and aired. It wasn't foul but many people had been there, people in very distressed conditions. We used to give the caretaker a hand and say to the children, 'We'll have a playtime now,' until school was ready.

The evacuees came every day from Hull in flat lorries and all sorts of things. All during the blitz they came, and our headmaster wouldn't let us go in straight away . They'd open all the windows to air it out because there'd been a lot of people in. So we used to be outside in the playground, and some of us older ones used to teach the little ones to read, while we were waiting to go in. We used to be sitting on the ground and they would have a little book. They had to keep us all occupied while they were getting the school ready.

When the evacuees came out of Hull some of them put up shacks and sheds and all sorts. I can remember my father coming home and saying to my mother, 'I've told some people they can come.' He opened the door and seven people walked in. They came to our house for a long time at night. They came and slept overnight and went back in the mornings.

My friend and I had to shake out the grey blankets which had been used overnight by the people who came to sleep in the school. We folded them up and put them under the benches in the cloakroom.

Hedon schoolchildren volunteered to spend four halfdays of their Christmas holidays helping move emergency rations. (See page 68).

1942 Feb 25th **I**	Stock arrived from Browns. No newsprint in the delivery. Unobtainable
1942 Mar. 16th **I**	2 Bags of coal delivered from W. Finner. Rest of order to come later.
1943 Jan 25th 26th **I**	I was absent today with a severe chill. I telephoned Beverley for help although ill, I returned to school as the Education Authority had no supply teacher available, and this would have meant leaving Miss Elletson to run the school single-handed.
Sept 4th	The school cleaner had made a brave effort to thoroughly clean the school premises during the holidays.
1944 May 12	Efforts are being made to obtain gifts of clothing and footwear for very necessitous cases. Shoe and boot repairs are difficult.

Class VII. Back Row: Dennis Markham, Eddy Newton, ----? Middle Row: Betsy Anning, Sylvia Ward, Kathleen Johnson, Peggy Horner, ----? Greenwood. Front Row: Peggy Lowe, Doreen Barmby, Josie Scott, Barbara Jackson, Doreen Lowe, Kathleen Charlton.

Class VI. Back Row: Phil S. Courtney, Fred Mablethorpe, Roy Hall, Francis Birch?, Harry Thompson, Ronnie Smales. Middle Row: Mary Laidlaw, Kathy Easton, Eveline Cook, Jean Martinson, Eric Raven. Front Row: Dorothy Green, Jane Hurd, Mary Watkinson, Mavis Taylor, Hilary Palmer, Ethel Harrison.

May 23rd

1940

The East Riding County Council Emergency Committee have asked me to take charge of the Air Raid Precautions Services for Hedon and to act as Sub. Controller of Civil Defence for the Hedon Sub. Control Area. What is required to be done has been outlined to me and in view of present war conditions and the situation locally as it has been placed before me, I have agreed to undertake the work, subject to the Consent of the East Riding Education Authority.

Jan. 4th

1944

A.R.P. and Civil Defence. Refer to entry on May 23rd 1940. The duties as outlined there have been carried out by the Head Teacher to this date. Now a Senior A.R.P. Officer has been appointed who will relieve me of the administrative and clerical part of the duties and who will be responsible for maintenance and training of personnel and care of vehicles. The operational duties will be carried out by me as Sub. Controller, whenever required, as heretofore, by night or by day. The number of alerts has been 808, and the number of incidents 539. These duties are being carried out in a voluntary capacity.

The Defences

Barrage Balloons – great big ugly things, weren't they.

One of the barrage balloons came down. I saw pieces of silver-like rubbery material, black on one side and silver on the other.

Seeing the barrage balloons going up was frightening because you knew the bombers were coming when they went up.

Where I lived, we had a barrage balloon at the back of us. We used to get perks like sweets from them. They were good to you on the barrage balloon sites.

There were searchlights at Paull at Battery Cottage. Sometimes we were allowed to go out and see all the searchlights but not often.

You could see the searchlights, like fingers moving round the sky – I can see them now in my mind.

There was a searchlight on Paull Road and it got this plane in its beam and the plane came straight down the beam and one, two, three, four, a stick of bombs, and the fourth one hit the light.

Oct. 17th

1939

Air Raid Warning at 11.0 a.m. Rehearsed plans immediately put into effect. About 70 scholars at the school, after the remainder had been sent home. All the staff remained. All Clear received at 11.50.

Oct 24th

I

Very poor attendance in the afternoon. following air raid warning. Attendances cancelled.

Nov. 22nd Air Raid Warning 7.15 to 8.20 last evening.

Jan. 11th

1940

Air raid sirens tested at 11 a.m. in the district. Air Raid drill carried out at the school in conjunction with the Infants' School.

	Mixed	Infants	
On roll	222	85	
Present.		49	
Remaining in Air Raid	51	21	
Remaining, absent today.	27	9	} 108
Not present since war began	11	—	
Rarely " " " "	21	—	

It has been arranged with the Infants' School to hold air raid drill each Thursday morning at 11.

I've seen planes at night when they'd got the searchlights on them. I used to stand outside at night and watch them. First one would get them in the searchlight, then two crossed. Then the guns fired. They did shoot some down. You could see searchlights all the way along the Humber.

We used to watch the searchlights trying to converge on the planes and then the guns would start up. The guns on Magdalen made a heck of a lot of noise. They had rockets on the aerodrome – they sort of swished. We used to go out of the shelter if it was 'quiet'. We could see the guns firing . The searchlights used to pick up the planes and you could see puffs of smoke as the shells burst round them. They never seemed to hit anything.

The sound of the guns firing was earth shattering – a tremendous noise. They were at Magdalen Camp and on the airfield. We were very frightened.

My father used to take us outside to look at what was going on. Sometimes the sky was red with fire over Hull and the guns flashing.

They had rockets on the aerodrome – hundreds of them. They used to go 'Wheeooosh!' – like that. It used to frighten me to death.

The guns on the aerodrome made a special sort of noise – I've never heard anything like it in my life.

There were Ack Ack sites at Magdalen, Preston and Paull and rockets on the airfield. Now, when they all opened up, you didn't know if they were bombs or guns.

There was an Ack Ack battery on Preston Road. A bomb dropped right on them. I remember a train coming to take these coffins away with all Union Jacks on them.

I'd been out playing one evening and the sirens went and the searchlights. The guns went off and I was absolutely terrified and ran home.

We used to think we could tell the different aeroplanes from the sounds they made. We used to say, 'Oh, yes, that's a Jerry', but whether we were right or not I don't know. Sometimes when my father wasn't there we'd look out and see the planes in the searchlights and the guns firing at them.

The Ack Ack guns on the airfield used to fire right across Hedon. Some people were frightened of them and moved away.

June 20th 1940	Very severe air raid during night — 11 children came to school, some of them arriving as late as 10.30 a.m. Did not mark the registers in the morning.
I	
June 20'	Attendances cancelled 37/221 after night air raids. for the morning only.
June 26	Severe air raid last night. Until further notice, or instructions from Beverley, I have arranged with the parents that if the "all clear" siren goes after midnight, school will open in the afternoon only. 3 children came to school this morning Have sent them home until after dinner.
I	
	Air raid warning from 4 a.m. to 4.40 a.m. School commenced at 10 o'clock. Another air raid warning at 10.5 a.m. to 10.20 a.m. Children taken to shelter. A third air-raid warning at 12.45 p.m. lasting until 1.7 p.m. Many children came late to afternoon school. Registration not completed until 1.45 p.m.
I	

Air Raids

In the first year or so of the war the Germans used to mount daylight raids, usually carried out by a single aircraft, or only a few planes. By 1941 they had changed to night attacks and it was in that year that the heaviest raids took place.

Although numerous bombs, mines and shells landed all round Hedon and buildings on the outskirts had windows broken and tiles removed, in Hedon itself there was only one serious incident, when a landmine dropped on Burstwick Road (Magdalen Lane), destroying four houses and a bungalow. Twelve people were killed and seven injured. The extent of the damage and casualties from that one mine shows just how lucky the town was not to have had more direct hits.

The Luftwaffe used high explosive bombs which had a thick casing, to produce shrapnel as well as blast. Sometimes they attached sirens to the fins to increase fear and these were known as screaming bombs. Landmines were cylindrical containers about 15-feet long and two-feet six-inches in diameter, carrying, a very large amount of high explosive and capable of causing much blast damage. The casing was comparatively thin and they were dropped by parachutes. They would not fit in the bomb bays so the planes carried two, one under each wing, for balance. Incendiary bombs were about two-feet long and made of thermite and magnesium. They were carried in canisters which sprang open when released from the planes scattering them around. If accessible they could be easily dealt with, but could cause problems if they landed on high roofs or places difficult to reach.

1940
July 1st.

I

There was an air raid this morning at 10.30. I took the children into the shelter. Gun fire continued until 11.15 a.m.

At teatime another air raid took place over Saltend ^^^igniting a tank^^^ and several families

later presented themselves at school asking to be allowed into the shelter. As they were in a terribly nervous state fearing the explosion of other tanks from the heat, they were allowed to enter. They left the shelter at 3.30 the next dawn.

July 2nd.

At 8 p.m. this evening about 30 people presented themselves at school asking for the shelter to be opened so that they might get their children and themselves comfortably settled in case of an air-raid. I explained to them that this could not be allowed until the siren was sounded. Luckily no siren, and no bombs throughout the night.

In 1943 came the butterfly bombs. These were anti-personnel bombs and were dropped in batches much like the incendiary bombs. However, these had metal 'wings' and fluttered down to the ground, hence the name. The action of hitting the ground left the bomb primed and on a hair trigger, which could be detonated even by the vibrations of someone walking past. Although only small, they were lethal to anyone setting them off, and the difficulty of finding and dealing with large numbers of these caused much disruption. A copy of a warning poster showing a picture of the bomb is on page 49.

A further hazard was our own anti-aircraft defences. What goes up must come down, and the nose cone and base plate were particularly heavy pieces of metal. Even if the guns were successful there was always the risk that the shot-down plane might land on your head. Quite a catalogue of potential dangers!

There was a big tank full of water, in case of fire, at the back of where the Post Office now is. It had barbed wire round the top. It was very big.

It was difficult to find your way in the blackout. One very dark night my father had come home and gone into the kitchen and found people eating their supper. He'd only gone in the wrong house. Fortunately they knew him.

On my way home from school an aircraft came over and everybody was saying it was one of ours. All of a sudden its bomb doors opened and it dropped a load of bombs on Hedon Aerodrome, which was covered with old cars to prevent an enemy plane landing. The next day 'Lord Haw Haw' came on the wireless and said that Hedon Aerodrome had been bombed and many aircraft destroyed on the ground.

'Lord Haw Haw' was William Joyce, who broadcast in English for the Germans on programmes beamed directly at Great Britain. He had a distinctive upper-class drawl and began his programmes, 'Gairmany calling. Gairmany calling.' He often quoted local information designed to make people think there were spies everywhere. Whilst people were worried by his broadcasts at first, he quickly became a figure of fun, being mimicked and parodied by many comedians. After the war he was executed as a traitor.

Early on in the war, I was playing outside when there was a big bang. I ran in and went upstairs, and looked out of the back window – we were directly opposite Saltend – and the smoke was oozing up into the sky. It was just one bomber. I could see it plain as day. I could see a small dot which must have been another bomb, and then another big bang.

The barrage balloons went up and the sirens went one day and they bombed one of the tanks at Saltend. We were standing out at the front and my mother said we weren't going to bed that night because the bombers would come back, because they would be guided by the light of the fire. I can remember the fear of all the adults who thought, 'That's it – Saltend's going to go up tonight.'

I remember one of the tanks at Saltend being bombed. I remember getting up to look at it that night. The sky was just red.

I used to be in the Ambulance Service. One night we were called to Saltend following a raid. It was very dark and we were stopped at three road checks just on the way from Hedon. It took us ages to get there, and then we had to bring back a casualty. He was bleeding badly and someone had applied a tourniquet. I travelled with the injured man in the ambulance and I was supposed to loosen the tourniquet every so often to avoid cutting off the blood supply altogether. At the same time I was not supposed to make it so loose that he bled to death. There was no light in the ambulance and I had to do this in the pitch dark. The short

July 5th **1940** **I**	Morning school abandoned after last night's air raid. The L.E.A's rule of opening school at 10 a.m, if the "all clear" siren goes after midnight, was received today. I shall put it into force on Monday July 8th
July 15	The Local Education Authority issue notice that school will Commence at 10 a.m. when the sirens blow after midnight
July 18th **I**	Air raid warnings from 7 am. to 7.45 am. Some children came to school at 9 o'clock, but others obeyed the 10 o'clock ruling. (See page 195 July 5th)
July 22nd	Air raid warning from 11.50 pm to 1.20 am. School Commenced 10 am.
July 23rd	Air raid warning 1.20 am to 3 am. School Commenced 10 a.m,
July 30th	Air raid warning 12.10 am to 1 am. School Commenced 10 a.m.
Oct 1st **I**	School Commenced 9 am inspite of raid warnings during the night. New regulations have cancelled the 10 o'clock arrangements

42

journey seemed to take ages but fortunately we got him back and he was alright. After this they gave me a small bicycle lamp.

We went to see Saltend when the oil tanks got hit. It was in the afternoon. There was smoke billowing up into the sky for ages.

I remember the bombs going down the searchlight in Paull Road, because I actually saw them going down. It was one of the biggest in the area and got planes nearly every night. They bombed and machine-gunned it and some of the soldiers were killed. All the cows in Mr. Jackson's field were killed as well, good job they weren't people.

The plane came straight down the searchlight and dropped four bombs. When the fourth one exploded the light went out.

There was a stick of four bombs dropped on the searchlight. They were screaming bombs. I thought I'd had it that night. Horrible!

There were some bombs just over at Sheriff Highway – screaming bombs. I remember them coming down. They made a devil of a row. They were designed to frighten people.

I could tell the difference from the sound between a land mine and a bomb. You could also tell from the sound which was a German plane and which was one of ours.

After an air raid, when the all clear went we used to come out of the shelter and stand on the wall near the fish and chip shop and we could see Hull docks on fire. We did that many a time.

I used to wish a bomb would drop on Hedon School. I used to hate school.

My dad was outside. He didn't often come in the shelter as there wasn't any room for him. We were a big family and we had neighbours in too. He was fire-watching for incendiaries.

Every call there was, my dad used to belt out, leaving me, my mother and my sister. We used to sleep in the shelter but it was wet and we had to pump water out. That was an existence, that was.

My father was not at home during air raids. He was a part-time fireman and got called out when there was an alert. During the war, the Auxiliary Firemen had a place in George Street. It was one of George Head's stables. They used one of his wagons. When it came in, they used to clear it, and load it up with hoses and a ladder and hitched on a U.P.A. – that's a pump. Len Sharpe was the only full-time person there who kept records and things. They used to get the warnings first. When one came in a runner was sent out. All the firemen had a bell and he pressed these and they all ran to the station to be ready for anything that happened. Later it was the N.F.S.

A landmine cap landed on an outbuilding near us. We were under the table. It made a big thud and our windows cracked.

Incendiary bombs fell in our garden, all round the air raid shelter and the chicken house. My father and the wardens put them out with sand and a stirrup pump. The chicken house was a bit charred.

My dad was a Special Constable and, after a raid was over, he would bring Mr. Cox in for a cup of tea. Mr. Cox was up, fire-watching at the school.

We lived in Church Lane. We watched from the front door. We could see the landmines and thought they were going to drop on the Town Hall. One went up Burstwick Road. It was on

Nov 14 1940

The air-raid siren was sounded twice this morning. School nurse continued her duties in the shelter. The dripping roof was a great source of annoyance to us all.

The L. E. A's regulation, advising that children be sent home on the warning signal ^air-raid if the end of a session is near, was carried out this morning. Parents seem to be against the measure. I am writing to parents asking for their opinions, and shall keep the children in the shelter during the lunch hour if I find that parents are worried about their children being in the streets

I

Nov. 15th

Parents wrote this morning asking that their children be kept at school during the air-raid warning if this occurs near dinner time

I

Feb 4th
" **5**th
1941 I

Air raid warning 1.20pm to 1.30pm
"   "   "   2pm to 2.50pm.
The cold in the shelter is intense.

a parachute. The night before, Delma Spicer had slept in our shelter. She was a friend of my sisters and she was killed.

My father came rushing in as he'd seen a landmine coming down. I was poorly with measles and couldn't go into the shelter so they shoved me under the bed.

Geoffrey Spicer sat next to me at school and he was one that died and his sister Delma used to come and play with us. Strangely enough, we accepted this as part of the war. I don't know why. This was possibly a child's attitude towards it. You see, we also knew people who'd lost people in the army.

That morning in school after the bomb dropped on the Spicers – I can remember that morning going to school. We were all very sad and horrified really to think the day before how the Spicer family was all there and next day they had all gone except one.

A landmine dropped in Burstwick Road. We were sleeping in the garden shelter and felt the ground move when it dropped. We seemed to be lifted up in the air. My grandfather came round at two a.m. to make sure we were alright. None of our windows were broken but most of the shops had to be boarded up.

I used to do a paper round before school. On the morning the Spicer family was killed I went to have a look. All the emergency services were there and the men shouted at me to go away. When I looked at the wooden bench opposite, I saw it was covered with pieces of bodies and I ran off.

When the bomb dropped on the Spicers' house and Josie Ellerton was killed as well, I really felt scared. Until then the war had been exciting and a bit of an adventure.

When the bomb dropped on Burstwick Road all our windows went in, and in the field at the back of our house I remember seeing all bits of clothes and things.

We only lived in George Street but our windows were not blown in, but those in the Market Place were, which were further away. It's funny how it happens.

I wouldn't get up when the siren went, but when the bomb dropped on Burstwick Road that decided me – I dived under the table!

The night the land mine exploded, the pictures came down, the soot came down, the windows came in – terrible! My sister wouldn't get up for air raids but she came crawling out that night.

One night, when we'd stayed in bed instead of going to the shelter, we heard such a bang. It was such a bang. All the house then – it was dislodged a bit – the skirtings and things like that – you could see it – all the locks went and you couldn't open the doors. After that we used to get smothered in cockroaches. When you came down on a dark morning they'd go. You didn't come down in your bare feet in the dark. My mother kept putting various powders down and eventually got rid of them. Ugh!

Josie Ellerton and her mother were killed and her father was blown into the toilet and he was saved. It was uncanny.

There was an awful sort of stillness after the bombing down Burstwick Road and there were casualties. That was a bad night.

I had the job of taking the policeman who had lost his wife – he knew his wife and his son were dead – I had the job of taking him back to the Alison Hall. He wasn't injured, not

Mar 19th **1941** **I**	Severe raid last night over Hull and district lasting nearly nine hours. Only 34 children attended this morning.
May 8th **I**	Last night severe air raid in this district. A parachute mine demolished 4 houses in Hedon. 1 of the scholars named Edward Spicer is under the debris, feared killed.
May 8th	Severe raid last night Delma Spicer, Geoffrey Spicer, Nick Spicer, John French, all scholars, lost their lives by enemy action. David French rescued injured. Many incidents.
May 9th	Severe raid last night. Incidents.
June 2nd	Closed for Whitsuntide - two days.
June 2nd	School repaired after damage to ceilings.
May 9th **I**	7 children came this morning 23 " " this afternoon. Another devastating air raid last night was the cause. Hedon and district was pounded by heavy bombs.

physically – but mentally – and I thought, 'What can I say?' – and all I could do was put my arms around him . There was nothing you could say: you were too full yourself. Nothing seemed adequate.

Despite being up all night (I was in the Ambulance Service), I went to school the next day. I felt I had to go: I would not be beaten. I was a pretty filthy mess by morning. I was as black as the ace of spades. I met S. T. Johnson going in and he said, 'Oh, you've come. Well go home and get changed and come straight back!' It didn't hurt me, and some children had turned up so I was needed.

My brother was a lorry driver before he got called up and, when the bomb fell on Burstwick Road, he was one of them that helped to clear all the rubble and move the bodies. This was an awful job to do because he was only young at the time.

We weren't far from the mine on Burstwick Road. Our garden was full of paper and suchlike. In fact there was even a concrete gate post blown over into our garden. It blew our windows out and the lock off the door. We were all in shelter at the time. It didn't half bump. I could tell it was a landmine and I can remember saying at the time, 'There'll be another one yet', because they always carried two. There never was, because the other one didn't go off.

Although we were nearer the bomb we didn't lose any windows, but my grandmother did, and she lived further away.

I remember walking up there in the morning – course I do – ooh! It was terrible, terrible – just a heap of rubble. There were a lot of rescue workers – firemen, rescue, A.R.P., all of them.

Opposite Holyrood house where Mr. Harness lived was the mortuary. All the people that got killed were put in there. It was converted stables, specially done for the war.

When the bomb dropped near the Boulevard everybody was evacuated. We came to my grandmother's house and then the next day we went to Welwick for a week so I couldn't go to school. It was quite an exciting time really.

At the same time the mine landed on Spicer's another one landed near the back of Birkholme. It didn't explode and 90 people had to be evacuated. There were so many unexploded bombs that it took the squads several days to come round. However, there were some naval officers billeted at Birkholme and they came out and did it. The next morning I got the base plate off it but my mother made me take it back. A lot of people didn't come to school at that time.

After the Boulevard was evacuated they all stayed with friends and relatives around the town. We had a houseful. Everybody used to help everybody else.

We lived in the Market Place and, after the bang, when the mine dropped in Burstwick Road, everything seemed to go quiet. Suddenly all the windows out of the Co-operative shop, which was there, fell – all one after the other – all crashed out. Funnily we didn't lose our windows.

We lived in the Market Place and our windows were blown out.

After the raid, I can see the Co-op windows now. They just put little tiny squares of glass in the middle and the rest was boarded up.

Mar 31st	Loss of school hours during the year April 1st 1941 — Mar 31st 1942 due to air raids is as follows:-
I	
1942	

April 1st	23 minutes
April 2nd	43 minutes
April 14th	9 minutes
June 10"	13 minutes
" 12th	10 minutes
Oct 7"	20 minutes
" 24	17 minutes
Nov 3rd	61 minutes
10th	80 minutes
12th	34 "
Dec 12th	17 "
" 22	25 "
Jan 13th	43 "
Feb 2nd	27 "
Feb 5th	12 "
Feb 6th	1 hour 43 minutes
" 17"	30 minutes
" 18	62 "
26	13 "
Mar 3rd	16 "
" 9"	8 "

There was glass all over the Market Place. A lot of windows were blown out including ours at the back.

Butterfly Bombs

We had a talk about butterfly bombs at school because they were very, very dangerous.

The other big scare was when the anti-personnel bombs dropped on Burstwick Road. It's the only time I can remember all the kids doing as they were told. They were frightened to death because one chap had got off his bike to pick one up and was killed.

Mr. McKee was my grandfather. He was cycling to work when he kicked a bomb or hit it with his pedal. It exploded and he was killed.

Oh, that was a scare. It was a Mr. McKee. He worked up at Magdalen Farm. He was going up the track in the morning and he picked one up and it blew him up. Then they sent in a load of sheep to clear some of the fields with a dog. The sheep were all right but the dog got killed. We were told not to go up there.

My brother worked at Forkerleys Farm. Usually, my dad who was very reliable for timing, got us up. This day, for some reason or other, he was late. My brother normally cycled to work with Mr. McKee but this day he missed him. If he had been on time he would have been with him when the bomb exploded. I've been thinking about it – it makes you wonder – perhaps it was the hand of God.

I'd just left school and we were loading for George Head at the station yard. The Police came and said, 'George, can you take your wagon and pick Mr. McKee up?' We went and

49

June 6th **1940** **I**	Received from Kirtons — first aid materials. Received 18 enamel plates + roll of lancaster cloth. Last night's air raid caused a serious drop in attendance this morning. Only 47 out of 82.
July 30th 1940 "I	Air raid warning 12.10 am to 1 am. School commenced 10 am. Janet Sturrock came an hour late. Did not give her a mark
July 31st **I**	Heard this morning that Janet Sturrock was knocked down by an army lorry; yesterday on her way home from school.
Feb 6th **1941** Feb. 18th	Spent nearly 2 hours in the shelter during afternoon. Severe gunfire. 3 times in the shelter today
I July 4 **14**	We have 88 children on the roll at the beginning of the school year. Severe air raid over Hull last night. Shrapnel rained down in our streets during the early hours of this morning. There was a poor attendance at the morning session.

collected him. He'd been killed by a butterfly bomb. The army got tanks and ran them up and down the fields to explode the bombs because they were anti-personnel and didn't damage tanks.

It was about 7.30 when Mr. McKee was killed. We heard the explosion.

There were leaflets put up about anti-personnel bombs – not to touch them – after Mr. McKee died.

The Ministry of Defence came to school and told us not to pick up pens or pencils or anything strange because it could be a bomb.

A chap called Tom Fox was going along the track with a pair of horses and a load of corn. He pulled off to let the postman pass and kicked a butterfly bomb which went off and killed him. The horse had to be put down. They cut the corn with a Bren gun carrier with a binder behind because you couldn't see the bombs in the corn.

I particularly remember being told to leave things alone because of the anti-personnel bombs. People used to get their arms blown off and things. We used to play in the fields round Hedon and we were told, 'Don't pick anything up that looks attractive!' They warned us about this at school.

In harvest time the dogs were sent into the corn first in case there were any butterfly bombs. The police said we had to watch out for them.

Shrapnel

I used to go collecting shrapnel. I used to be able to sell a small piece for sixpence. It was alright at first but later on there was so much around that nobody would buy it.

When there'd been a raid during the night we used to go out looking for bits of shrapnel – girls as well as boys.

There were some landmines came down over the Haven and we went and got bits of cord off the parachute and bits of shrapnel. I kept it for a long time.

We collected bits of parachute from the landmines, bits of shrapnel and the nose cones off shells.

I went to look at the land mine which didn't go off. It was stuck in a field, you know, and the parachutes – they were massive parachutes, all blue silk.

We got material from parachutes and if you could get enough people made underclothes of it. I think it was silk – white silk – and you didn't need any coupons.

A mine dropped near Forkerleys Farm and we went to see this crater. It was about 30-feet deep and the hole went to a point. Terrible, those landmines.

We used to go shrapnel collecting – swaggering as to who had got most of it and the biggest lumps. Shell shrapnel and bomb shrapnel. Oh, we had a big store of it.

I can remember those big jagged lumps. After a time, you could find it anywhere, and nose cones, and bits of shells.

During the summer time we walked to Paull. There'd been a lot of mines dropped and we were going to collect shrapnel – and there were all these horses dead in a field. There were big craters in the fields all around.

P.T

Nov. 10"
1939

Hockey for the girls, football for the boys, and country dancing for the intermediate girls are now sources of interest in school life.

Dec. 11"
1944

Mrs. Gee and Mr. Cox are remaining after school on many evenings for country dancing training with the senior scholars

"Dig for Victory"

Jan. 19"
1940

Negotiations with the Hedon Corporation on the granting of the use of land for extra school garden. Letter also received from the L.E.A. on this subject.

Feb. 13"
1940

Further Correspondence on the extra school garden Suggestions, with County Hall. Problem fully discussed with members of the staff Concerned and various plans Considered

May 20"
1940

Extra lessons taken in gardening by senior boys and girls this week at the two allotments taken over by the School for production purposes.

How We Did Our Bit

We were good at English and good at maths because you had that every day, and scripture.

We had sewing and music and geography and history. We did a lot of singing. We had a school hymn. We always sang it at assembly on Mondays and Fridays. It was, *He who would valiant be*. You can get fed up with something!

We were taught the National Anthems of all the Allies. We did a lot of singing – the French and the Canadian – I can't remember them all now but I can still sing *the Marseillaise*.

One day Mr. Cox and another teacher sang a song called, *Travelling Down from Bangor*. They took their false teeth out to do it so they looked very old. We all laughed and I have never forgotten it.

We used to sing *Greensleeves* and I still can't stand it.

We did quite a lot of singing. We learned all the National Anthems of the Allies. I liked the French one best.

We didn't do much singing – there were two or three of us – they barred us. We were out of tune and disrupted the rest of the class. We used to go into another classroom and read or something.

In the war a lot of Free French soldiers came and Mr. Johnson invited some of them into school. They used to sit in on some of the lessons, and also tried to help with a few phrases of French. Mr. Cox was interested in it all as well. They had come here with nothing at all. They hadn't even a flag or anything. So a flag was made. It sort of went to a point, in three

Maypole dancing was a prominent school activity. Seen here on Market Hill.

1939 Sewing and Knitting

Sept. 19th Needlework record for 1938-9, with proceeds of sales amounting to £10-2-6, sent to the County Treasurer today.

Nov. 2nd This week the needlework stock has been sorted and shared, each teacher of a needlework group receiving what is needed for the work for the term

1940

April 12 Knitting of garments for the Navy continued.

Collecting

Jan 8th Scholars are collecting silver paper for the Lord Mayor of London's appeal. They are also bringing contributions to purchase wool for knitting garments for all old scholars serving in H.M. Forces.

1944

June 8' Closed in the afternoon for the visit of the East Yorkshire Regimental Band to Hedon on the occasion of "Salute the Soldier" week. Special savings effort throughout the school during this week.

colours and in the middle the Cross of Lorraine was embroidered. They said everybody , all the boys, even if they only did one stitch, had to join in. Even the male staff did.

Before the French went we had to learn the French Anthem at school, so, as they were going, we could all sing it to them on Market Hill.

With Mr. Cox we did Morris dancing and Maypole dancing even though it was wartime. Oh yes, we enjoyed that.

We used to do Maypole dancing and all our P.T. on Market Hill in our navy blue knickers and white blouses.

Even though it was wartime we still did our Maypole dancing. It was lovely going to all the big houses in Hedon. We went to Mr. Lambert's, that's the New Hall, and to the Todds at Birkholme.

Mr. Cox taught us *The Lambeth Walk.*

We did our P.T. on Market Hill and we had to keep away from Windy Ridge because they didn't like children. We did it in our knickers, nearly down to our knees.

I remember playing netball once on Market Hill and the Russians stood all round the pitch watching us, all the way round.

Girls' P.T. Class on Market Hill
Back Row: Barbara Panton (now Pockley), Valerie Barmby (now Johnson), Jean Ketley (now Farrah), Nita Anning, Frances Birch, Joyce Gardner (now Barker), Pat Mosley, Rita Bell, Kathleen Macnamara (now Ellis). Barbara Easton (now Redmore).
Middle Row: Johnson?, Edith Wallis (now Robinson), unknown?, June Smith (now Martin), Florence Shields, Margaret Rosindale (now Isaac), Joan Macnamara, Eileen Andrews, Edna Tong (now Williamson).
Front Row: Alma Wright, Barbara Tong (now Gray), Betsy Anning, Topsy Atkinson, Phyllis Newton.

1940

Feb. 9th | The scholars are collecting silver paper for the Lord Mayor of London's Red Cross Fund;

and are bringing weekly contributions for the school wool fund, for knitting for H.M. Forces.

April 12th | 28 lbs. of Silver paper Collected at the School. and despatched to the Lord Mayor of London.

Potato Picking

Oct. 2nd Closed for the potato picking season
1942 to October 16th.

Sept 6th | Requests from farmers for assistance in
1943 potato picking and farm work. All available Cards issued to volunteers, over 12 years of age.

Oct. 8th | Closed for the Autumn holiday for two weeks. Most of the older scholars have finished their agricultural employment.

July 10th | Twelve Senior scholars on potato picking
1944 under permit for Mr. H. Johnson.

I suppose we did do our lessons but we seemed to have more free time. It didn't seem as though they bothered us so much. The teachers still gave us our lessons but they seemed much more relaxed.

I especially remember learning a new hymn called, *Fair waved the golden corn*. It made a big impression on me because the weather was very beautiful at the time.

We used to dig for victory. We grew vegetables in the school garden. The soil was beautiful because it had been dug so often. We sold the produce in school. The Town Council gave us manure. Some of the boys used to go on farms potato picking in the autumn.

Where the school is in Ketwell Lane now, the boys went there and did gardening. They used to go to Bilton for woodwork and the girls to Withernsea for cookery but it had to stop when the war started.

We used to have to march from Market Hill School to the gardens. You were doing gardening for learning. It was good stuff that we grew. It had to be done properly.

Some of the boys used to do gardening and some of the girls were chosen to help dig for victory. They had to choose partners and I was chosen first by one of the boys. I was very embarrassed.

Whilst I was helping with the gardening, one of the lads picked up a worm and chased me with it. The teacher was very cross and said I was silly to be afraid of a little worm. She sent me back to school.

The girls used to have to help in the allotments, they were down Westlands way. The sun had baked the earth like I don't know what. The tools weren't any good. It was absolutely hard and you couldn't get a spade in it. I don't remember much being grown there!

We used to take socks with holes in them to learn how to darn them because you couldn't throw socks away, and we knitted squares for blankets. I used to hate sewing.

When we started knitting, the first thing was, you had to knit a dishcloth. You had to get it right before you could move on. I had to keep doing it again and again. I don't remember knitting anything else. The teacher said to me, 'You're supposed to be using white,' and I said, 'Miss, it was white when I started.'

I was in Miss Farnaby's class. Mr. S. T. Johnson also had a desk in that class room. He was the headmaster.

We learned to knit while the boys did gardening.

We had saving stamp books. We took so much a week and got stamps and that bought you a saving certificate when you got 15/-.

I might have knitted a scarf if I'd got my brain in gear.

Some of the older boys had to do fire watching. Three of us at a time used to sleep in the school. Mr. Cox was in charge. We had camp beds in the class where there was a big stove. They taught us how to put out incendiaries with a stirrup pump and sand.

They taught us how to use a stirrup pump at school, just the older ones. We had a shovel with a real long handle to put sand on incendiary bombs. We practised on Market Hill.

We bought savings stamps and stuck them in little oblong cream books and when you had enough you got a certificate.

Although not organised by the school many of the children took part in concerts put on by the Misses Elliott. We believe one of the Misses Elliott was second from right in the middle row. The Mayor, Councillor Tinkler, is towards the left.

Another of the Misses Elliott's concerts.

I used to take the money after it had been collected to the Savings Bank. For three years I did that – I must have done that from quite young. I took it on Tuesday mornings. I had to go to Miss Mitchell's every Monday morning with 10/- of copper. She had a sweet shop near the Town Hall. I don't know when she used her copper because I never saw anyone go into the shop. She used to give me five toffees – they were usually soft! This was after we'd collected the milk money on a Monday morning.

Miss Beedham used to go round the town collecting for the Red Cross. She had lodgings in Hedon and went home at weekends

We all used to save bits of silver paper for the Lord Mayor of London's collection. The girls brought bits of wool to school to knit things for servicemen. They did a lot of knitting.

We used to go collecting hips and haws for making rose hip syrup. We got paid for them at a shop in Baxtergate. The syrup was given to babies for Vitamin C.

We used to collect silver paper for the war effort. We collected rose hips as well; I seem to think we collected acorns also. It was maybe for the pigs. We used to take the rose hips apart and shove them down people's backs and, by, they did itch.

We collected silver paper and cardboard. Some of the girls who were good knitters made socks for servicemen. I was a terrible knitter so I had to do squares for blankets.

We collected rose hips on Far Bank for rose hip syrup.

I can remember collecting newspapers. We were allocated Sheriff Highway which was also known as Paull Road. We used to take them to the back of the Assembly Rooms.

We collected rose hips for syrup. We used to go down Paull Road because there were lots down there. We used to take the seeds out. They were horrible if you got them shoved down your back.

Another view of the Girls' P.T. Class.

The following is the certificate portion and photograph:

B.F.C.6.

The St. John Ambulance Brigade
CADETS

This is to Certify

That ....PRIMROSE.W.EGERTON.... Age ....

of ...Hedon........ **Cadet** Nursing...........

Division, County of ...East Riding of Yorks.......

No.VI...District, has attended an examination in........

.........A.R.P.............and has satisfied the

Examiner.

Jane Berrow R.R.S.
Examiner

Date of Examination 7/10/43 ....
Commissioner

Note.—Certificates in three additional subjects will qualify for a Cadet Proficiency Badge.

The St. John Ambulance Brigade Cadets
One of the activities for girls was the St. John Ambulance Brigade Cadets. The Certificate above is of particular interest as, although issued by St. John's, it shows that Primrose Egerton had been examined, not in First Aid, but in A.R.P.
Those in the photograph are: Back Row: Ethel Harrison, Pam Brockman, Margaret Taylor, Beryl Rennardson, Betty Morrell, Norah Lloyd, Lilian Fewlass, Primrose Egerton, Ethel Thompson.
Middle Row: Kathleen Macnamara, Mrs. Wickens, Mrs. K. Epworth, Mrs. Morrison, Mrs. Rate, Mrs. B. Miller, Gwen Betts.
Front Row: Margaret Macnamara, Beryl Courtney, June Smith, Margaret Bogg.

Some Other Activities

We used to play whips and tops, marbles, skipping and ball games. There was a sort of season each year for these things.

There were railings round the Bull Ring on Market Hill. We used to go climbing on them and doing tipple-overs.

We played block, a kind of hide and seek, but one of our best games was jumping dykes – if you fell in you didn't half stink. Then you got it in the neck from your mam. We know we shouldn't have done it but some of us used to climb on the school roof when nobody was there. It wasn't half steep.

We did a lot of skipping. We played rounders and ball. We made up our own games. On Sundays all the family went out for a walk or a picnic and we played cricket.

We had a stock of blankets for emergency use in our house and they nearly filled one room. My friend and I used to crawl in there and play on them.

Even though it was war time, things were a lot freer in those days and most of us could go wandering off without our mothers worrying. We usually managed to get home for tea. There was plenty of open space and with all the troops and guns and lorries there was plenty to see.

During the war my father was away. My mother never let me roam around very much. We used to stay in our own community.

We had about six different routes to school. It depended on how much time you had. We'd even go back on ourselves and come back down Church Lane. Sometimes we'd watch Mr. Markham, the butcher, killing pigs. His back way came on to Church Lane. I don't think anybody in Hedon went short of meat during the war.

There was no traffic much then and no petrol for most people so it was much safer going to school.

The school dentist used to come. He had a face like a Co-op tea-cake with the jam scraped out.

In the autumn you could go potato picking. There was a special holiday from school and you got paid for it but not much. Your mam used to take most of it off you.

In September we would go brambling and my mother would make blackberry and apple jam. You got extra sugar for it.

If we went out on the bus anywhere we had a special song to sing on the way home but we couldn't go anywhere very much. I can remember all the words:

> Hedon, Hedon, here I come,
> Mr. make your engine run.
> Down the High Street, 49 Street,
> Where someone waits for me.
> I'll take a bus ride, now and then,
> To Saltend Pier and back again,
> But H.E.D.O.N. spells
> Home sweet home for me.

When it snowed we played snowballs. I remember one boy threw a hard one which hit Mr. Cox right in the ear and he was off school.

Lilian Fewlass (now Swainger) and Kathleen Macnamara (now Ellis) with the 'Red Cross Pig'.

Fund raising to buy an ambulance for the Red Cross as part of the War Effort. The children had presented envelopes containing money which they and their friends had raised. The marrow was the champion in a competition and the photographer asked the children to gather round it. The function was held in Mr. Tinkler's garden at The Cottage in the early part of the war.
Adults: Mr. Tinkler, Mr. Warn. Mrs. Tinkler.
Children: Ken Ablett, Francis Ellerton, Mary Watkinson (now Johnson), Beryl Rennardson (now French), Sylvia Ward (now Wilkinson), Hilary Palmer (now Woodford), Roy Rooney.

At the beginning of the war we used to go up Blueball Entry at the back of the Town Hall and fill sandbags. We had to deliver one to every house in Hedon for putting out incendiaries. We did it at night and weekends.

On our way to school we used to pass a pigsty and this pig used to jump up and put its head and its legs over the front. Sometimes it crossed its legs. It was real friendly, just like it was talking to you. Somebody told us it belonged to the Red Cross and was going to be raffled for the war effort.

There used to be a sale for the Red Cross – I always remember going. It was in a paddock on the left down Station Lane and they had a sale there of sorts. Then they went into the yard where Harry Harness lived. They were selling all sorts of knick knacks. George Waite bought half a stone of apples and oh, he paid such a price for them, but he didn't mind because it was all for a good cause.

At the Red Cross fêtes they had a sort of competition. They had a piglet and it was all covered in grease. They put it in this square and if you could catch it you won and could have it. Nobody could ever hold it but it was fun watching people try.

We didn't do many concerts for school but the Misses Elliott, who lived at the top of Church Lane, were into these things and were always arranging them.

My cousin and I used to go to Miss Ridley's dance class. We used to do it in the Alison Hall. We did tap dancing.

The school gave concerts in the Assembly Rooms. I sang a duet, *The Keys of Heaven*. I didn't like the boy I sang with. He was a refugee from Hull.

We had these concerts from time to time we used to go to. Stan Register was the comedian, he was very funny. Doreen Macnamara played the accordion and Ernie Sharpe was a ventriloquist.

Although at that time there was a very active women's Red Cross, we were in the St. John Ambulance Brigade Cadets. We learned first aid and got various badges. We also learned about A.R.P.

I went to the St. John's. If they wanted to practise on anybody, it was always me. If they wanted to put a sling on, or bandage anybody, it was always me. I was very young at the time.

They used to have these dances at the Assembly Rooms. Doreen Macnamara played the accordion, Len Sharpe on drums and Mrs. Underwood thumped on the piano.

When I was older I was allowed to go to the dances at the Assembly Rooms. Five shillings I think it cost if there was a supper on. There were all different nationalities, mostly officers who went. You'd be dancing around and you'd try to say something and they'd stop in the middle of the floor and get a phrase book out.

The Free French came to dances in dress uniform. Some of the girls wore long dresses even though there was a war on.

Sometimes on a Saturday night there would be a fight and someone would be knocked down the stairs.

I got 7/6 a night for playing the accordion. When Len Sharpe was away, Mr. Hunt used to play the drums.

1942

July 31st

I

School closes today for summer holidays, but reopens each week day for milk distribution at 10.30 a.m. (5 weeks)

1942.

The distribution to the scholars including the Infants School was in the hands of Mr. Cox and the Head Teacher.

Sept. 7th

A British Restaurant has been opened by the Town Council and the children can take a hot mid day meal there for 4d cost to the child. Today is the first day for the children and at the request of the Ministry of Food, the children will attend from 11.45 to 12.15. With the consent of the Education Authority school hours are altered as follows. 9.0 to 11.45, 1.0 to 3.45. Two teachers daily attend with the scholars and help to serve them. This is on a voluntary basis on the rota system.

1942.
Oct. 23rd

The British Restaurant has on an average 65 children each day for dinner.

Food and Drink

Our milk at home was delivered from a churn into a jug but at school we each had a little bottle with a cardboard top.

Sometimes if the sirens went there would only be about five of us at school and there was all the milk delivered. One day we set about drinking the milk out, to see who could drink most, and went home sick as dogs. (Boy)

If there'd been an air raid after a certain time, we could go into school late. I think it was after midnight or one o'clock. We could go into school about ten o'clock. Sometimes only a dozen of us went and the milk bottles all came, so we drank the milk. I can remember drinking three in the morning and three in the afternoon. (Girl)

I didn't like the milk but we made pom poms with the cardboard tops. We wound old wool round for ages just to amuse ourselves.

Potato Pete

Sometimes, after an air raid, there weren't many of us, so we used to drink the extra milk. It was really thick and creamy. I used to love it, but now I hate it. I haven't drunk it for ages.

In winter the milk was often frozen and we used to stand it near the stove to thaw out.

In the summer holidays they opened the school every day, so we could go for our milk. At first lots of us went, but it got too much to go every day just for a bottle of milk.

I used to be the milk monitor. We used to have to collect it off the wagon when it came. It was only in small crates. Then we carried them into school and shared them round. We took it in turns.

Before the war, it was normal practice for people to go home and eat their main meals at midday. This consisted of a main course and a pudding, usually something substantial such as suet, sponge, pie, or sometimes rice. This applied to most of the children, the exceptions being those who lived too far away to get home and back. When the war came, many of the menfolk were away and more women went out to work. The Government encouraged the setting-up of works canteens and British Restaurants to cater for the smaller businesses. Shortly after the Hedon one had opened it became the custom to take the children there. At the end of the war it was financially not viable and was going to close down, but the Education Committee took it over solely for use as a school canteen.

1943

April 27 Now that the school canteen is in operation and available to all children, fish and chip dinners and packed lunches are no longer allowed at the school in the dinner period.

Nov. 29 School times for the winter months are 9.15 a.m to 11.45 a.m and 1.0 P.M. to 3.30 P.M. The morning session is at 9.15 instead of 9.30 to allow the quarter of an hour at 11.45 instead of 12 noon to enable the children to attend the Hedon British Restaurant for a hot meal, if they so desire.

Dec. 1st Prices for children's meals at the British Restaurant have been increased from 4d to 6d for a dinner of meat and vegetables and pudding.

1944

Jan. 3rd Milk in ⅓ pint bottles, arrived from Riley's Ltd. of Hull, as usual. The number of bottles is 132.

1944. Jan 3rd No. for British Restaurant. 32.

66

My friend, Ethel Harrison, and I had to collect the dinner numbers from the teachers, and the money. We had to take it to the British Restaurant and pay Mrs. Roberts, the cashier. She gave us tokens to take back to school but, on the way, we used to go to Ethel's house, next to where the British Legion is now. Her mum always had a cup of cocoa and a scone ready for us. When we got back to school we used to say we had to wait because Mrs. Roberts had been busy.

I usually went home for dinner but sometimes I went to the British Restaurant. I thought it was a real treat; I really enjoyed the food. People didn't go out for meals very much in those days so it was different. Mrs. Ford was the cook.

I have stayed but I didn't like it. I was choosy about what I would eat.

In the British Restaurant there was a counter on the left, where you collected your grub. After the war it became the school canteen. The food was quite palatable – it wasn't the Ritz or anything like that – but it served a purpose. It helped out with the rations and it gave the children a hot meal. I think it was a good thing.

I didn't often go to the canteen. When I did go I didn't like it particularly.

My mother used to work there , voluntarily, doing the dinners. When my mother was working, I used to go there for dinners. We had different coloured tokens for different courses. The dinners were brilliant.

When it first started it was called the British Restaurant before it became the school canteen.

The dinners weren't bad really. I can remember having rice pudding.

Dinners – we had to go down to the British Restaurant. The meals were very good – we had puddings with like an orange syrup. Mrs. Ford, the cook, was very good. She did all sorts of things. They used to get tins of pork from America and that was very good as well.

I didn't like school dinners one bit.

Before the British Restaurant was a canteen, I used to go to the fish shop, Farr's it was, and take the fish and chips back to eat at school. If it was very cold, the teacher who was supervising us made us a drink, if we'd taken cocoa and sugar with us.

I didn't stay at school for dinner, but I used to make cocoa for those who stayed in and had sandwiches. I did it where the cloakroom was, where we went in.

Sometimes I used to take sandwiches for dinner and they made us a cup of cocoa. It was real dark, horrible, strong.

I took sandwiches for dinner but on Tuesdays and Fridays we went to the fish and chip shop. We used to take Oxo to school and boil a kettle to make a drink. We had little milk bottles with cardboard tops. You pushed the middle in to open them.

I never stayed at dinner time because I had to go and take my granny her dinner. She lived in one of those cottages down Souttergate. My mam packed it in a basket and I took it to her.

I went home to dinner. We had an hour and a quarter. There was plenty of time to get home and eat your dinner. It was getting back – messing about or playing marbles or something like that. You'd get into trouble for being late then.

I used to go home for dinner and, if we had any money, on the way back, we used to put

During the War, emergency rations were stored at several places in the town. Some four tons of these were stored at The Cottage (home of Mr. Tinkler) and in 1942 these had to be removed to the New Hall (home of Mr. Holmes Lambert). The picture shows a party given for the children who assisted. Back Row: Valerie Barnby, Doreen Lowe, Gordon Hudson, Sheila Saunders (now Dickinson), Mary Millener (now Carr; who worked for Mr. Holmes Lambert and had made the trifle), Geoffrey Smith and Barbara Easton (now Redmore). Front Row: Peggy Lowe, Ethel Thompson, Phil Courtney, Primrose Egerton (now Gray), Alex Shann (with the bowl), Fred Mablethorpe, Kathleen Easton.

twopence in the fag machine, which was on the Post Office – it's where the bathroom shop is now – hung on the wall. Twopence for two cigarettes and three matches. We used to have a drag in the lavatories at playtime. Sometimes we got caught and then you got the cane from S.T. We had to come home for our dinners or we couldn't have got the fags.

We always had lots of animals, pigs, chickens and things. I remember the pig being killed. We didn't go short of food.

My dad's business took him round the farms and sometimes he was given eggs or some butter.

When you look at what the rations were, two ounces of this and two ounces of that, I don't know how our mothers managed. If she got word that Tong's were going to have some bananas, an extremely rare occasion, she'd be down there like a shot.

There were a lot of gardens and allotments in Hedon and many people grew their own food.

Some of the children from the school helped to move the emergency rations. Mr. Tinkler had been looking after them and when he died Mr. Lambert had them. The children walked in a crocodile with these big boxes. I can remember making a party in Mr. Williams' house (Mr. Lambert's assistant) to thank them. They had sandwiches, sausage rolls, pop and tea. I made a huge trifle in a big old fashioned bowl. There was a picture and a piece in the paper about it, but they never mentioned that I'd made the trifle.

We helped to move big boxes of food from Mr. Tinkler's to Mr. Lambert's house. I think they were emergency rations. We were given a party afterwards and received a letter from Lord Woolton, Minister of Food.

Under the stairs we had some very big tin boxes full of ships' biscuits, corned beef, probably powdered milk as well, sort of iron rations, for use in case of emergency, such as an invasion, or heavy bombing. They were distributed in a few different places and I think this was in case one got bombed.

A newspaper photo of the children who helped to carry the food from the Tinklers' was taken on the staircase of New Hall. It was sent to America for American children to see what we were doing.

Miss Mitchell's goody shop was at the end of the street. We used to spend our coupons there, but you didn't get many sweets. She was very fair though – she never let you down.

Mrs. Marlow had a baker's shop next to the Town Hall. I went there sometimes and got a cake to take back to school for dinner. It smelt really lovely in there.

Next door to the Town Hall was Mrs. Marlow's shop. She was a one-man band. You could go into the shop from the street and you could see right down, into her kitchen, and she had a big coal oven. Beautiful, the stuff she made. She was a good baker. You could go in and buy a bun at dinner time.

Mr. Tinkler, who was the mayor, used to have do's in his garden at The Cottage. They had one to raise money to buy an ambulance for the Red Cross. We had all been having little sales and things and we had to present the money we had collected. There was also a competition for the best marrow. I don't know who won but when the photographer came to take the picture he told us all to gather round, so we all got our picture taken.

1944

Feb. 29 Winter school times discontinued and normal time resumed. The period before 12 noon for reaching the British Restaurant in good time is reduced to five minutes, as the adults do not now attend so early, and the number has decreased. The price for a child's meal is now 5ᵈ instead of 6 d. without any reduction in quantity or quality. This is in response to a request by the Head Teacher to the Hedon committee. From 50 to 60 scholars attend the Restaurant daily and the teachers give voluntary help and supervision each day on a rota.

1945

March 26 Arrangements are in hand to take over the Hedon British Restaurant as a school canteen.

1945.
April 13ᵈ The school canteen opened on Tuesday with dinners at 5ᵈ per head. Average attendance for the week is 48 daily from this school. The Infants' School also attend.

A Royal Surprise

An unexpected omission from the School Log Book was any mention of the drive through Hedon by the King and Queen. None of our contributors is quite sure when it was and there was some confusion as to which way they were driving. It is hardly surprising, as this was not an official visit to Hedon, and timing and routes of such visits were kept secret in wartime until the last minute. However, we have received confirmation that they were travelling south, from an old boy of Sproatley School. The children there also went out to see them pass, driving towards Hedon. Council minutes give the date as 1 August, 1940.

My mother somehow found out that the King and Queen were coming through Hedon. She flew down to school to tell them. At first the teachers didn't believe her. We all went out to see them. I can remember exactly where I was standing. They only rode through but we lined the street and saw them.

We went out of school and stood outside Painter's Cottages. The King and Queen drove through with three or four other cars. They came from Preston and slowed down and waved. There were a lot of officers in the other cars and I thought Churchill was with them. We had a super view of them.

The King and Queen drove through Hedon from Preston and we all lined up outside Painter's Cottages. There used to be a big stone on the corner of Sheriff Highway, and my mother said to us, when we got back home, she stood on there and could see very well. They drove fairly slowly past.

I was only very little and our class sat on the double pavement edge on Souttergate to watch them come past.

I was off school at the time, but word went round and everybody was outside. I stood in the Market Place and there was a policeman walking up and down and he said, 'I wish you'd all buzz off. There's nothing to see', and just then the King and Queen came past and we all waved.

I thought they would be wearing crowns and was disappointed when they were not. They were just wearing clothes like ordinary people.

They just drove slowly past. Mind you, we were stood outside for ages waiting for them, and they just went past in a few seconds. It all seemed a bit of a waste of time.

We went out of school down Souttergate. It must have been in 1940 because I'd left by 1941. We stood behind the shelter and we had a real good view. They went from Hedon towards Preston.

It runs in my mind that these cars were not expecting to see us. We stood outside Painter's Cottages. When they came into Hedon they were coming quite fast and had to slow down very sharply when they saw us. They slowed down and they waved to us. They must have been coming from Preston because if they had been coming the other way they would not have had to slow down.

We came out of school through the shelter, into Souttergate to see the King and Queen. We lined the route. They waved to us as they went past. They were going towards Preston.

They came from the direction of the station in a big car. We were standing in the Market Place.

When the King and Queen came by, we went out to see them. We waited a long time and then they just drove past. At least it got us out of school.

It was a great thrill to see the King and Queen as we'd only seen them in pictures before and they waved to me.

Road-block on Haven Bridge.

Soldiers and Camps

There was always something going on. There were lots of soldiers here.

At the beginning of the war, many British troops were stationed in the area to train for action and to man the anti-aircraft defences. As the war went on, these were added to by a variety of nationalities: the Free French who came with the fall of France, Italian prisoners, who were given a great deal of latitude following Italy's surrender in 1943, Russians (prisoners or displaced persons), and, at the end of the War, German prisoners and those of their allies in Central Europe. Huts were built on various sites but particularly down Ivy Lane and along 'Cali'. ['Cali', short for California, is the local name for West Lane, the continuation of Ivy Lane].

My dad was the sort of person who brought them all home. My mother never knew who was going to turn up next.

My mother used to help run a canteen for soldiers at the chapel. Lots of soldiers came and W.A.A.F.s from the barrage balloons and A.T.S. from the anti-aircraft sites. Some came by lorry from as far away as Little Humber. They ate loads of toasted tea-cakes. Three soldiers who always stuck together were nicknamed, 'Faith, Hope and Charity' behind their backs. They found out about this and when they went away they sent a card signed, 'Faith, Hope and Charity'.

At Christmas there was a regiment of soldiers in the town and they made toys. They made a toy for every child in school (Infants School). One of them dressed up as Father Christmas and presented them all. That was jolly good of them.

We used to hear them on Market Hill because the camps were all up the lane. They used to come to Market Hill to do their drills.

The army people used to go to the Assembly Rooms and they'd painted the walls with sort of scenery all the way round, and black figures of people like a frieze.

Some of the Free French were very pleasant but there were a lot of Arabs among them. Some were down Sheriff Highway with their tanks in the field, where Spencer Close now is.

The Free French were very handsome. It was the uniform I think.

We had French, Italian and Russian as well as English soldiers and they never bothered us at all.

Our house used to be full of Free French. I had two older sisters and there was another lass who lived with us.

Opposite where the cemetery is now were all these army huts – all along there up to Styche's Orchard.

We got the French there and they used to give us things as we were going by.

The officers used to be in a house opposite the Shakespeare, next door to St. Anthony's House in Baxtergate

There were always loads of soldiers in Hedon. I mean the girls who were a bit older than me, they had a whale of a time. I wished I was a bit older at the time but now I'm quite pleased I wasn't because I'd be older now.

The Mayor, Mr. S. T. Johnson, takes the salute during 'Salute the Soldier Week'. With him are commanders of the British and French troops stationed in the district. The aim was to raise funds for the war effort.

One of the few photographs we have been able to trace showing the Nissen huts down Ivy Lane. This photograph was taken at an Armistice Day Parade sometime after the war.

The Free French used to give girls Crosses of Lorraine made in brass.

There were all kinds of soldiers in Hedon – Free French, Russians, Italian prisoners of war, displaced persons – all sorts. The Italians bought bikes for £2.50 from Len Sharpe. They wore brown uniforms with big yellow patches. The Russians came by train to Hedon. They once gave a concert on Market Hill singing, with instruments made out of tin cans and things. They made toys to sell and cut people's hair to make a bit of money.

Italian prisoners used to come and do gardening. They made lots of things. For a long time I had a basket they'd made. They were very helpful. My mother used to swear by them.

I think with all these men in uniform around, I was just a little bit too young.

The P.O.W.s made toys and things. The Russians used to go singing in Hedon. They sang *The Volga Boatmen*. They were good singers.

Ivy Lane was beautiful when the Italians were there. They decorated in front of their huts with bright stones and glass.

There were Nissen huts under the trees. There were a lot of Italians here. They used to ride bicycles round, a stupid sort of thing to remember, but they all seemed to have their knees and feet pointing outwards when they were riding. We thought this was rather peculiar. Perhaps the bicycles were too small for them. The Italians were more obvious because they were darker.

So many of those in the huts were Mongolians and Russians. They used to march round Hedon and sing and I've seen them dance. They collected glass and stones and made all these marvellous decorations outside their huts. I can remember them dancing, how they did the dances, you know, Cossack dances, on Market Hill.

Some Russians came to our house. They were very young and couldn't speak much English but they used to sing round the piano. They were very good singers. They used to say, 'Volga, Volga', for *The Volga Boatmen*

Some of the prisoners of war used to come to our house to get a bath. They were very friendly.

The prisoners were camped near school so we saw them a lot. I used to be a bit afraid of them.

We used to do Maypole dancing for the prisoners. They appreciated anything you did for them.

Once when I was walking home I thought some Italians were chasing me. They hid behind gateposts. I ran like anything – really terrified.

The Italians used to have camp-fires and sing-songs down 'Cali'. We used to go and join in. One called Toni cut our hair. They were a right friendly lot.

They used to take the Italian prisoners in lorries to work on farms and we used to pelt them as they went past.

They made all pavements out of broken bits of brick and slate and what have you, down Ivy Lane. It was quite a sight to see.

My dad sold some bikes to them during the war. All the soldiers had bikes. In fact everybody had bikes.

Acrobatic model made by an Italian prisoner of war. The acrobatic lady is made of perspex from a crashed aircraft. She performs somersaults when the wooden side pieces are squeezed.

The exterior of the School has little changed. Photograph as it is now.

The Russians came by train one night and they used to sing, absolutely fabulous. They used to march all round 'Cali' and we used to go and see them. They left just overnight as quickly as they'd come. Later on someone told me they'd all been sent back to Russia and been shot.

The prisoners made toys, these pecking chickens and acrobats between two pieces of wood. You nipped the ends and they turned over. They made rings out of pennies. You gave them some cigarettes or something for them.

The prisoners down Ivy Lane made little gardens. They kept it really nice. It was lovely down there. They used coloured stones and things and made patterns. We used to go and look at them. I think it was to make it more like home.

They used to buy bits and pieces for their bikes from old Mr. Sharpe – brake blocks and things like that.

I can remember some Russians playing football. The children were also playing on the green. They kicked a football hard and it hit a child. They were so upset – they really tried to comfort the child and apologise.

Some of the soldiers, I think it was the Russians, used to stand outside Sharpe's garage with a rifle and a blanket over their shoulder. They wouldn't let you walk behind them.

One of the prisoners went berserk. He was an Italian. He just went crazy and they took him away.

They made all sorts of toys – fantastic – like two pieces of wood with cotton through with a dolly on. You squeezed the sticks and they used to spin over. If you took them a shilling or a coin they'd make you a ring. They did it to make a bit of money.

The prisoners made cigarette cases out of aluminium, and lighters too. I don't know where they got it from – perhaps crashed planes. Some of them were very handy.

We used to go to school across 'Cali'. We used to love going across to school because there was Americans there and they used to give us chewing gum and chocolate, dark chocolate.

Down Ivy Lane it was lovely. The prisoners made pictures outside all the huts, made of stone and broken glass. We used to go for a walk on Sunday nights to look at these things. They were lovely patterns on the floor.

They used to regularly march from Ivy Lane to Johnson's garage with their towels for baths, down the Market Place along the main road.

Somewhere I've got some brushes made by the prisoners. They also made things like toys and lighters. They were clever really.

I had a bracelet made out of a spoon. It was all chased with fancy patterns. It was lovely really. I gave it to my daughter.

At the end of the war the prisoners were allowed quite a lot of freedom. Some of them came to chapel.

When the German prisoners were there, there were some Roumanians amongst them, one called Peter, who wrote to me later, and one called Heinz

May 1st 1945 | All the black-out curtains, wire netting and wood frames, and the protective woodwork in the girls' porch have been taken down in the holiday by the Head T. and Mr H Cox and stored in the air raid shelter. The brickwork covering the porch windows has also been taken down and the bricks stored in the air raid shelter. The windows of the screens and classrooms have been scraped with the help of Senior boys and the school cleaner, who has done extra cleaning and scrubbing as well.

May 4th | Average attendance: — 84.4.

" 8th | V.E. Day. School closed.

" 9th | V.E. plus 1. School closed.

I 10th | School re-opened after victory celebrations

" 28. Sept I | F.K. Baldry called to collect tea boiler used for A.R.P. purposes.

April 1st 1946 | Mr. F.D. Lacey, who left this school to join H.M. Forces on Oct. 23rd 1939, has been demobilised and resumed his duties here this morning. He takes the Top Class.

Victory Days

When the war in Europe ended on 8th May, 1945 (V.E. Day), there was a spontaneous celebration and two days public holiday. Most people expected the war in the East to continue for some time, with heavy casualties likely to be incurred in storming the Japanese homeland. They were very relieved when it was quickly brought to an end by the dropping of atomic bombs on Japan on the sixth and ninth of August. The Japanese surrendered five days later on August 14th. Again a public holiday of two days was decreed, which was observed in a similar manner to V.E. Day. The official victory did not take place until June 8, 1946, in order to allow time for as many members of the services as possible to return home and be demobbed and a more organised celebration to take place. The East Riding Education Committee resolved in April 1946 to make no provision for the victory celebrations to be held on June 8 saying this was a matter for the local councils. Whilst people can remember the things they did, understandably, they cannot always clearly remember which celebration it was.

V.E. Day street party on Church Lane.

Victory Day – 8th June, 1946. Fancy dress parade on Far Bank. left to right: Barbara Johnson (clown), Sylvia Ward (with elephant), Mary Laidlaw, Bob Parker, Geoff Barrow, John Hudson, Lilian Fewlass, Hilary Palmer, Francis Ellerton, Kathleen Macnamara. Nobody remembers the elephant's name!

Victory party, Lambert Park Road. Joyce Gardner, top left, Mrs. Farr, top right.

I remember us dancing in the Market Place. It was at night and there was music.

I think there was a Sports Day and a Fancy Dress parade on Far Bank.

I remember dancing on Market Hill and the street parties. I can't remember having a party at school but we got a holiday.

Churchill came on the wireless and said the war was ended. Everybody came into the streets and talked to everybody – all excited. We had two days holiday. It was great.

There was a party on the field where the balloons were. There was a marquee and we had sports.

There was a fancy dress party at the Alison Hall but I don't think we had a party at school.

Everybody celebrated in the Market Place, dancing and cheering and the rest of it.

On V.E.day we had dancing in the Market Place – lots of people came. It was lovely. They came from all over. We were allowed to stay up. It was great and it was on our front too. They had music and lights and eats. It was a good party. We had another do on V.J. Day as well.

There were some fantastic parties – people got food together somehow. We had a party in a Nissen hut at the back of the houses on Sheriff Highway. There was a big party in Lambert Park – there were tables from one end of the road to the other. Absolutely fantastic!

We had a victory party in Church Lane. We borrowed trestle tables from the chapel and brought out chairs. We went round everybody and everybody contributed something. It was all arranged in just a couple of hours.

We had a party over Far Bank way. We had a holiday from school.

When V.E. Day came, oh! it was great. Everyone was so excited and relieved. ALL the people were in the Market Place. It was packed. There was singing and dancing and food and drink. It was wonderful. We had a dance on the Market Place and a tea. We had trestles on the cobbles and after tea they had this dancing. Everybody helped one another to get food. Thinking back I don't know how my mother managed on the rations. I think it was Wally Everingham supplied the music, but I'm not sure. It was loud for those days.

There was a BIG CELEBRATION.

They had all sorts – dancing in the Market Place. They went to great lengths with everything. They put flags up. Even my mum was out on the street. She wasn't really that sort of person, but, she was so overjoyed the war was over, she joined in.

Hedon church was all lit up and people were dancing in the street.

There were three celebrations – one for V.E. Day, one for V.J. Day and one for Victory Day. They were all smashing.

We had a do and things in the Market Place – a dance – there was all dancing. It was full was Market Place; choc-a-block with people. Everybody was boozing but we weren't old enough. Everybody just came out. It was joyous.

All the main street was all packed. We were elated.

My Most Vivid Memory

We asked our contributors what was their most vivid feeling or memory of the war. The excerpts below are from replies to that question.

It was all those sirens going off. It was so frightening.

My father went away to the services and I was very sad, thinking we would never see him again.

I've never forgotten the number on my Identity Card, even after all this time.

I remember the feeling of being in a kind of limbo, and talking with my friends about what we would do when the war was over. We thought it would be a kind of magic time, when we could do anything or buy anything we wanted.

One Sunday morning about 1940, the Home Guard had been called out since two o'clock and everybody thought there was going to be an invasion. You could sense the fear in the grown-ups, everybody speaking quietly, and then three Spitfires flew over real low out to sea, and you could sense the relief that there was somebody there to do something about it.

I always think we were that little bit younger. We ought to have been that bit older, because there were an awful lot of soldiers in Hedon and we missed out on them.

It was an exciting time.

My mother was at the Control office at the Town Hall where the calls came in. I went there one day after school and an air raid warning came in while I was there. My mother asked Mr. Johnson if I could turn the siren on and he agreed. The worst of it was I managed to do the wrong thing and turned the 'All Clear' on. It was only for a few seconds while they put it right, but I can still feel the embarrassment.

The woman next door to us died suddenly in our air raid shelter. She was in the bed next to me. We had to get out and go and sit in the house.

There was a little fair on Market Hill. I was on a roundabout and an Italian prisoner got on behind me. I was horrified.

I was always very frightened. I was afraid when the siren went if I was outside in case I couldn't get home. I remember that.

Getting ration books was my most lasting memory. I wanted to have first go. We took them to the shop and got all those little pieces of lard and that. It was quite a thrill.

The noise of the guns – CRACK! CRACK! CRACK! – every night practically.

When you were a lad, you didn't think about it like you do now. To me it was exciting – watching searchlights and planes – and looking for shrapnel.

The night the screaming bombs came down. The searchlight was operating that night, it was only three fields behind us, and we really thought, 'Well, this is it,' because the screaming got closer and closer. The windows in our house were blown in.

There was a Red Cross sale in Baxtergate opposite Holyrood House and my father bought me a little puppy. People had given things to sell but I can still remember the feeling carrying that home.

The thing that I remember most was the guns. I mean there was on Magdalen camp anti aircraft guns all the time, and on the racecourse and I can remember going out of the shelter and watching the searchlights getting the planes in the searchlight and then they fired at them.

Some Italian prisoners used to sit on a piece of wood on the wall outside Morrison's fish and chip shop. One day when I was going past, somebody tipped them off and they fell down.

My brother was 13 years older than me. He had pigeons. He had hand-reared two of them – they were really tame and followed him all over. He had to go to the war and the police came and said that they would have to be destroyed because they weren't registered and if there was an invasion they may be of use to the Germans. We hid them in a cupboard but the police found out and my father had to kill them. I'll always remember how upset my brother was. It made a big impression on me.

We used to run to the shelter at home. We held cushions over our heads. I don't know what we thought it was for but we had a good laugh about it.

My most vivid memory was of flares over Magdalen. They put about three or four flares did the Germans and it was just like day. The flares were on parachutes and came down slowly but they just didn't drop any bombs.

The mine on Burstwick Road dropped before the siren went so we weren't in the shelter. Everything shook and all the soot came down the chimney. It covered everything and everybody. We dived under the table and listened for the other one, because they always came in twos, but it didn't go off. So we dashed into the shelter, a brick communal one, and only then did the siren go. A man came dashing in and fell through the curtain across the entrance. When he got up he looked just like a nigger minstrel and we all laughed.

Walking to school with my gas-mask.

We were in the shelter and my dad came in and said, 'All get out and look at this, because you'll never see anything like it again.' We all got up and lined up on the path. The whole of Hull was on fire. All you could see was just one great big fire.

When the guns were firing, you could watch the shells going up through the searchlights.

Miss Cass lived at my uncle's in Lambert Park. Her boy friend was away and once a week I was sent there to ask if there was anything from H.Q. On the occasions when I brought her a letter, we were ordered to carry on with our work whilst she read it. I can see her smiling now as she read her precious letter.

I was at my aunt's about ten o'clock in the morning. We heard a plane coming across and I just looked and three bombs were coming out. One landed in the field right in front of us and a massive cloud of soil came up. It broke the windows and we just flattened on the floor. It is my most vivid memory.

You know where Beckett's is, we used to go across there and go into the cellar. Oh, how I hated it! I hated it! My sister who was older than me, she wouldn't go in, but, oh! how I hated it. I did really. I can still remember it. Down those cellar steps – it was awful. You never forget.

Later on I was surprised how we'd all got used to the war and just accepted it. Now I would be terrified.

I went to Hull with my dad after a raid and seeing all those streets flattened. Ooh, you couldn't get down anywhere. It's a sight I'll never forget!

Always when Winston Churchill came on the wireless we had complete silence. It was amazing, wasn't it – the confidence everyone had in Winston Churchill.

My most lasting memory was of missing my dad. When he came back he wasn't the same person and neither was I. I regret missing those years very much and I still do.

I was walking down the road with my friend when a man came past us on a bike. He was wobbling all over and shouting to everybody, 'The war's over! THE WAR'S OVER!' We were all so elated and excited. It's difficult to put into words.

A boy's collection of shrapnel, including the striker and fin of an incendiary bomb, the fuse and base plate of an anti-aircraft shell, and part of a shot-down German bomber. The old penny gives some idea of size.

8th June, 1946

To-DAY, AS WE CELEBRATE VICTORY, I send this personal message to you and all other boys and girls at school. For you have shared in the hardships and dangers of a total war and you have shared no less in the triumph of the Allied Nations.

I know you will always feel proud to belong to a country which was capable of such supreme effort; proud, too, of parents and elder brothers and sisters who by their courage, endurance and enterprise brought victory. May these qualities be yours as you grow up and join in the common effort to establish among the nations of the world unity and peace.

George R.I.

A message from the King was sent to all schoolchildren. The Royal Coat of Arms is in colour and on the reverse are important war dates plus a space headed 'MY FAMILY'S WAR RECORD'.

Dec. 14 At 3.30 today the whole school assembled for the unveiling and dedication of the school War Memorial, presented by Mr F. Parker, of Hedon. A good number of visitors attended, together with the School Governors. The scholars sang suitable hymns and also Jerusalem. Names of old scholars who lost their lives are carved on the oak plaque. Mr. W. Rennardson of Hedon has executed the work.

1948

Hedon School War Memorial commissioned by Capt. E. G. Parker for the School in memory of the pupils who died in service of their country.

The memorial was left behind when the school moved to its new premises. It was subsequently rescued by Captain Parker's son, restored, and placed in the British Legion.

Photo by Dale Smith. With thanks to the Hedon Royal British Legion.

Appendix.

Wartime Staff Lists

Hedon Mixed School:

Class	1939	1940	1941
J I	Miss F. J. Cass	Miss F. J. Cass	Miss F. J. Cass/ Miss E. Herd
J II	Miss F. Farnaby	Miss F. Farnaby	Miss F. Farnaby
J III	Mr. H. Cox	Mrs. A. Andrew/ Miss M. Rennison	Miss M. Rennison
J IV	Miss M. Beedham	Miss M. Beedham	Mr. V. G. Skelton/ Miss F. J. Cass
S I (V + VI b)	Mr. V. G. Skelton	Mr. V. G. Skelton	Miss M. Beedham
S II (VI a + VII + Ex.VII)	Mr. F. D. Lacey	Mr. H. Cox	Mr. H. Cox

	1942	1943/44	1945
J I	Miss E. Herd	Miss E. Herd	Miss M. Gee/ Miss B. Dunwell
J II	Miss F. Farnaby	Miss F. Farnaby	Miss F. Farnaby
J III	Miss M. Rennison	Mrs. D. G. House	Miss M. Rennison
J IV	Miss F. J. Cass	Miss M. Rennison	Miss F. J. Cass
S I	Miss M. Beedham	Miss F. J. Cass	Mr. H. Cox
S II	Mr. H. Cox	Mr. H. Cox	Mr. S. T. Johnson (pending return of Mr. F. D. Lacey)

1946

J I	Miss F. Farnaby
J II	Miss K. Gibson
J III	Mrs. D. Mitchell
J IV	Mrs. F. J. Robson (formerly Cass)
S I	Mr. H. Cox
S II	Mr. F. D. Lacey

Hedon Infants:

	1939	1940	1943
Head:	Mrs. Ethel Smith Mrs. E. O. Grainger (Temporary)	Miss F. Rawle	Miss W. Albion (Mrs Pudsey)

Teachers:	1939	1942 onwards
	Miss N. M. Elletson Miss L. Stephenson	Miss N. M. Elletson Miss M. G. Robson

Acknowledgements

Maggy and Bob Cochrane thank the following, not only for their contributions to the book, but for the kind co-operation and the hospitality which they received, during their research.

Mrs. Molly Johnson
Mrs. F. J. Robson, née Cass
Miss N. M. Elletson
Mrs. Hilary Ketley, formerly Cox
Miss Valerie Spence
Mrs. Ann Agar, née Charlton
Mrs. Doreen Brewin, née Macnamara
Mrs. Mary Carr, née Millener
Mrs. Eveline Cook, née Cook
Mrs. Jean Crane, née Wilkinson
Mr. Gordon Cripps
Mrs. Sheila Dickinson, née Saunders
Mrs. Brenda Dixon, née Rosindale
Mrs. Kathleen Ellis, née Macnamara
Mrs. Barbara Gray née Tong
Mrs. Primrose Gray, née Egerton
Mr. James Hurd
Mrs. Margaret Isaac, née Rosindale
Mrs. Mary Johnson, née Watkinson
Mrs. Betty Longman, née Ward
Mr. John Markham

Mrs. Florrie Moore, née Doonan
Mrs. Jean Ogston, née Hall
Mr. Bill Panton
Miss Jean Panton
Mrs. Margaret Parker, née Taylor
Mrs. Barbara Pockley, née Panton
Mrs. Barbara Redmore, née Easton
Mrs. Kath Riley, née Brown
Mrs. Elsie Richardson, née Mannering
Mrs. Edith Robinson, née Wallis
Mr. Roy Rooney
Mrs. Lilian Swainger, née Fewlass
Mr. David Taylor
Mr. Harry Thompson
Mrs. Jane Thompson, née Hurd
Mr. Bill Tong
Mr. Harry Tong
Mrs. Valerie Uney, née Hobson
Mrs. Valerie Wigglesworth, née Robson
Mrs. Sylvia Wilkinson, née Ward
Mrs. Hilary Woodford, née Palmer

This is THEIR story

Special thanks are due to the present Headteacher, Mr. Paul Rimmer, and the Governors of Hedon County Primary School, for their co-operation in this project and to the Mayor of Hedon, Cllr Alan Bucknall, for helpful information.

Additional illustrations were provided by: Doreen Brewin, Brenda Dixon, Cliff Everingham, Barbara Gray, Primrose and Ken Gray, Molly Johnson, Mary Johnson, Hilary Ketley, Bill Panton, Barbara Pockley, Roy Rooney, Valerie Spence, Jane Thompson, Bill Tong, Valerie Wigglesworth and Hilary Woodford.